PLAYING AT NARRATOLOGY

THEORY AND INTERPRETATION OF NARRATIVE
James Phelan, Peter J. Rabinowitz, and Katra Byram, Series Editors

PLAYING AT NARRATOLOGY

DIGITAL MEDIA AS NARRATIVE THEORY

DANIEL PUNDAY

THE OHIO STATE UNIVERSITY PRESS
COLUMBUS

Copyright © 2019 by The Ohio State University.
All rights reserved.

Library of Congress Cataloging-in-Publication Data
Names: Punday, Daniel, author.
Title: Playing at narratology : digital media as narrative theory / Daniel Punday.
Description: Columbus : The Ohio State University Press, 2019. | Series: Theory and interpretation of narrative | Includes bibliographical references and index. | Summary: "Argues that digital media reveals much about core narrative concepts. Looks at games, web-based narratives, and algorithms in order to rethink narrator, setting, character, event, and world-building"—Provided by publisher.
Identifiers: LCCN 2019015297 | ISBN 9780814214084 (cloth)
Subjects: LCSH: Narration (Rhetoric) | Storytelling in mass media. | Hypertext literature—History and criticism. | Digital storytelling.
Classification: LCC P96.N35 P86 2019 | DDC 808/.036—dc23
LC record available at https://lccn.loc.gov/2019015297
Other identifiers: ISBN 9780814255506 (paper)

Cover design by Larry Nozik
Text design by Juliet Williams
Type set in Adobe Minion Pro

CONTENTS

List of Illustrations		vii
Acknowledgments		ix
INTRODUCTION	An Archaeology of Narratology	1
CHAPTER 1	Narration, Intrigue, and Reader Positioning in Digital Narrative	25
CHAPTER 2	Space across Narrative Media	53
CHAPTER 3	UI Time and the Digital Event	75
CHAPTER 4	Number and Movement in the Construction of Digital Characters	93
CHAPTER 5	Algorithm and Database in Possible Worlds Theory	121
CONCLUSION	Narrative Theory, Play, and Artifact	139
Works Cited		151
Index		161

ILLUSTRATIONS

FIGURE 1.1	Michael Joyce, *afternoon*	36
FIGURE 1.2	Scott Ichikawa, Thomas H. Crofts, and James Dvorak, *Outrances* (photograph)	44
FIGURE 1.3	Scott Ichikawa, Thomas H. Crofts, and James Dvorak, *Outrances* (posters)	45
FIGURE 1.4	*Morrowind,* narration from a guard character	47
FIGURE 1.5	*Morrowind,* player prompt	47
FIGURE 2.1	*Baldur's Gate*	55
FIGURE 2.2	*Mass Effect 2*	56
FIGURE 2.3	*Zen Bound 2*	56
FIGURE 2.4	*Tetris*	57
FIGURE 2.5	Roderick Coover, *Voyage into the Unknown*	58
FIGURE 2.6	Jason Nelson, *i made this. you play this. we are enemies.*	58
FIGURE 2.7	Lucy Anderton and Nicholas Robinson, *A Servant. A Hanging. A Paper House.*	59

FIGURE 2.8	J. R. Carpenter, *In Absentia*	68
FIGURE 3.1	Jason Nelson, *Game, Game, Game, and Again Game*	80
FIGURE 3.2	Ingrid Ankerson and Megan Sapnar, *Cruising*	85
FIGURE 4.1	*Uncharted: Drake's Fortune*	103
FIGURE 4.2	Hashtag use during 2014 State of the Union Address	116
FIGURE 4.3	*Understanding Video Games*	118

ACKNOWLEDGMENTS

AS THE INTRODUCTION will make clear, this book is very much the product of two intellectual communities: the International Society for the Study of Narrative, and the Electronic Literature Organization. The goal of this project is to reveal commonalities between these two scholarly groups, which have welcomed me in different ways into a generously and inspiring dialog on the relationship between narrative and digital texts. This book would not have been possible without the support of the many scholars I have met through the ISSN and ELO.

My argument has benefited greatly from the advice that I have received on parts of this project over many years. Back in 2011, David Herman provided extensive feedback on the topic of reader orientation in the electronic text that was the genesis of this project, and that has become chapter 1. Marie-Laure Ryan and Alice Bell made many suggestions on an earlier version of what has become chapter 5. Robyn Warhol and Zara Dinnen read and provided feedback on some of the material that became chapter 3. Although none of the writing that I did for the *Bloomsbury Handbook for Electronic Literature* became a part of this manuscript, the feedback that I received from Joe Tabbi and Robert Ryan on a chapter about narrativity in electronic media helped me think through many of the ideas that would form the basis of chapter 3. James Phelan helped to sharpen chapter 2 as the editor for *Narrative*. Along with Katra Byram, he also provided insight and advice about the whole manuscript as one of the editors for the Theory and Interpretation of Narrative series for Ohio State University Press. David Ciccoricco worked through many of the issues in this project with me. A generous invitation by Margie Luesebrink and Lai-Tze Fan gave me the chance to try out some of the ideas in chapter 4 at the Electronic Literature Organization Conference in 2017. Back home at Mississippi State, Peter De Gabriele and Eric Vivier made suggestions about theories of the crowd and multitudes that inform chapter 4. Throughout these last two years of reshaping and revising this manuscript, Kelly Marsh has been an invaluable sounding board.

My thanks to Sam Punday, an encyclopedic resource on video games and a deft provider of screenshots. And, as always, thanks most of all to Carol, who was willing to turn her life upside down to move with me to Mississippi.

An earlier version of chapter 1 was published as "Narration, Intrigue, and Reader Positioning in Electronic Narratives," *Storyworlds* 4 (2012): 25–47. A significant portion of chapter 2 was published as "Space across Narrative Media: Towards an Archaeology of Narratology," *Narrative* 25.1 (January 2017): 92–112. Part of chapter 3 appeared as "UI Time and the Digital Event" in *The Edinburgh Companion to Contemporary Narrative Theories*, eds. Zara Dinnen and Robyn Warhol (Edinburgh University Press, 2018), pp. 202–12. Chapter 5 was adapted from *Possible Worlds Theory and Contemporary Narratology* (2019), edited by Alice Bell and Marie-Laure Ryan, by permission of the University of Nebraska Press.

INTRODUCTION

An Archaeology of Narratology

THIS BOOK is about the relationship between digital media and narrative theory. There has, of course, been a rich if brief history of narratology's enthusiasm for and struggles with digital media. Early work in the 1980s and 1990s tended to be largely future-looking. Typical is the 1992 collection *Fiction 2000*, a book that "divines the prospects of fiction in the information age by examining cyberpunk literature," according to its back cover. A few years later, Janet Murray's *Hamlet on the Holodeck* (1997) was even more explicit in discussing the imaginary narrative forms that electronic media might make possible. Following almost immediately on the heels of these fanciful visions of future narrative were studies that tried to clear away the idealism surrounding digital media and take a rigorous look at the actual construction of electronic works. Espen Aarseth's *Cybertext: Perspectives on Ergodic Literature* (1997) and Lev Manovich's *The Language of New Media* (2001) have been particularly influential. Especially compelling has been the argument that work on these "new media" forms need to develop terms and categories native to the digital, and not to allow literary models to "colonialize" or otherwise warp our understanding of what digital media can do.[1] In the two decades since, scholarship on digital narrative has worked to disentangle itself from idealism about what

---

1. Essays by Aarseth and Eskelinen in the 2004 collection *First Person* are both influential and exemplary of the push for such a native approach to digital media, which is evident in Aarseth's work in founding of the electronic journal *Game Studies* in 2001 as well.

"future narrative" should be and instead begun developing more rigorous terms and frameworks for studying the way that digital media can tell stories.

This book is not, however, another in this tradition—or at least, not quite. Instead of offering an account of how we must adjust our narrative terms and theories in order to describe the storytelling potential of this new medium, instead I want analyze something broader: how narrative theorizing and digital media interact with each other.[2] In part I am hoping to explain why digital narrative has been such an important part of narrative theory in the last two decades. Although it is hard to quantify the impact that a particular medium has on narrative study, digital narrative has certainly seemed to prompt broader theorizing about narrative than some other "new" media like television and the graphic novel. More important is a larger question about how theorizing interacts with digital practice. Digital media are not natural creatures that exist in the wild, to be described accurately or inaccurately by a theory that comes along afterwards. Instead, digital media forms have evolved in a world inundated with narrative concepts. This book is an attempt to come to terms with this basic but messy fact. In other words, this book will ask how we can historicize digital media and narrative theory together.

MEDIA IN NARRATIVE THEORY

From the point of view of narrative theory, digital media has a special place within the discipline's hope to account for narrative across media. At least since the rise of structuralist narratology in the 1960s, narrative theory has taken as its explicit goal to develop models and terms that can apply alike to print, film, and visual art. Roland Barthes's famous opening to his 1966 essay, "Introduction to the Structural Analysis of Narratives" embodies this spirit: "The narratives of the world are numberless. Narrative is first and foremost a prodigious variety of genres, themselves distributed amongst different substances—as though any material were fit to receive man's stories" (250). The scholarship of the 1960s and 70s, the period now sometimes referred to as "classical narratology," explicitly embraced this cross-media focus. Seymour

---

2. In "Genre Trouble," Aarseth argues that "the computer is not a medium, but a flexible material technology that will accommodate many very different media" (46). This is definitely true in the broadest sense: the computer can function as a delivery system for music and movies, as well as a platform for games of all sorts. The degree to which it is best to see "digital media" as a singular or plural noun is not central to my argument in this book, and as a result I will refer to digital media in the plural while generally focusing on the qualities commonly (although not universally) shared among a wide range of individual applications of this computer technology.

Chatman's *Story and Discourse: Narrative Structure in Fiction and Film* (1978) performs an exemplary move by using a comic strip as an opening text to define narrative and set up the terms for the remainder of his book. The fact that Chatman expands the scope of his study to cover two primary media (fiction and film) is likewise typical of this evolution. We can see a similar media expansion in Mieke Bal's 1985 *Narratology: Introduction to the Theory of Narrative*, which gives significant attention to the generally neglected topic of narrative in visual art. As Jackson Barry wrote in 1990 about the rise of narrative theory,

> To someone based in a literature department this all suggests a magic broom that has gotten out of our hands to sweep imperiously into disciplines which our own disciplinary code of autonomy had let us ignore. Now narrative as a concept must seem to the literature professor oddly metamorphosed when it returns from the lips or pens of the social—and sometimes even physical—scientist. (295)

In the last twenty years, narrative theory has grappled more explicitly with the tension between the generalizing urge of narratology and appreciation for the specific features of individual media.[3] Of course, even within this classical period, there were lively debates about the degree to which narrative models can and should apply across media. Perhaps the best-known of these is between Chatman and David Bordwell on the narrator in film. In *Narration in the Fiction Film*, Bordwell offered a critique of structuralist theories of narration in film, and argued for the central role of viewer activity: "A film, I shall suggest, does not 'position' anybody. A film cues the spectator to execute a definable variety of *operations*"[4] (29). By placing the spectator at the center of filmic narration, Bordwell is able to discard the notion that there must be an implied narrator who is constructing the scene; instead, these "operations" are what create the narrative in the film. It is on this point that Chatman takes issue with Bordwell, arguing that it does not make sense to jettison the implied organizer of the film being viewed: "What does it mean to say that a film is 'organized' but not 'sent'? Who or what organizes it—not originally, of course, but right there on the screen during projection? Bordwell does not tell

---

3. Christine Brooke-Rose observes, "The initial excitements and fairly rapid disappointments of narratology must have had to do with the early high claims of universality. But the laws discovered, though often couched in learned words, rigorous analyses and diagrams, even mathematical or logical formulas, often turned out to be rather trivial" (283).

4. Throughout the book, all emphasis used in quotes is from the original text unless otherwise noted.

us" (*Coming to Terms* 127). Particularly noteworthy is Chatman's search for a definition of narration that is capable of encompassing the particular details of both fiction and film:

> I got into Bordwell's excellent theory in such detail because, except for our differences on the cinematic narrator, it is so close to my own. We both want to argue that film *does* belong in a general narratology; we both want to argue that films are narrated, and not necessarily by a human voice. We differ chiefly in the kind of agency we propose for the narrative transmission. (130)

Chatman's theoretical struggle to find a model for narration broad enough to account for both media is, of course, commonsensical and represents the long-running structuralist goal of creating models that can apply to any form of a given activity. This search for ever-increasing applicability, often through a move towards greater abstraction, is of course part of the appeal of Saussure's distinction between signifier and signified—terms that account for any signification regardless of the form that it takes. He was offering a *general* linguistics. That same spirit animated the work during narrative theory's classical period. Writing in 1989, Mieke Bal specifically criticizes this urge towards generality:

> In addition to making unwarranted claims about the generalizability of structure and the relevance of general structures for the meaning and effect of texts, such a construction [of narratology as the quest for a "perfectly reliable model"] would presuppose the object of narratology to be a "pure" narrative. Instead, narrative must be considered a discursive mode which affects semiotic objects in variable degrees. Once the relation of entailment between narrativity and narrative objects is abandoned, there is no longer any reason to privilege narratology as an approach to texts traditionally classified as narratives. ("The Point" 730)

Bal's questioning of the necessity of these general and ever more abstract structuralist models is the motivation for a turn to what David Herman called "postclassical narratology" in 1999. As he explains, "Postclassical narratology [. . .] contains classical narratology as one of its 'moments' but is marked by a profusion of new methodologies and research hypotheses; the result is a host of new perspectives on the forms and functions of narrative itself" (2–3). Roy Sommer has described this transition more recently as an emphasis on the pragmatic context of narrative analysis: "While the search for universally applicable definitions of narrative and narrativity or structuralist analyses of narrative mediation concentrated on 'what' questions and 'how' questions, postclassical narratologies appear to be increasingly interested in the 'why' questions that situate narratives in their pragmatic contexts. Such research requires transdisciplinary collaboration." In their 2010 collection Jan Alber and Monika Fludernik characterize Herman's book as a moment of "diversification" while advocating for a "second phase, which is one of both consolidation and continued diversification, [when] one now has to address the question of how these various narratologies overlap and interrelate" (5). In other words, the postclassical movement away from a structuralist or formalist understanding has opened up narrative theory to a variety of methodologies and disciplines. There has been some debate about whether the postclassical movement is an actual break from formalist narratology or more of an evolution,[5] and there remains a strong urge to look for ways to consolidate these methods into broadly applicable models and terms that retain some of the spirit of classical narratology.

The central urge within postclassical narratology is an appreciation for how our theoretical framework shapes the narrative models that we develop. Among other things, this has led to a subtly different understanding of the place of media within narrative theory. A particularly important milestone of this shift is the collection *Narrative across Media*, edited by Marie-Laure Ryan in 2004.[6] As she remarks, "In a period of swelling interest in both comparative media studies and narrative [. . .] the question of how the intrinsic properties of the medium shape the form of narrative and affect the narrative experience can no longer be ignored" (1). The overall goal of this collection is to explore this relationship between a medium and its effects, rather than to transcend these effects in search of more general theoretical models and terms. In his contribution to the book, David Herman posits two propositions, that "narrative is medium independent" and "narrative is (radically) medium dependent" before offering his synthesis: "the medium dependence of stories is a matter of degree" (51–4). In her introduction, Ryan particularly emphasized the idea that different media have different "affordances" for narrative. She explores

---

5. Gerald Prince remarks about these sort of assertions of a postclassical break: "But these explanations may be overly crude, this story overly dramatic. Perhaps, as suggested above, the change from classical to postclassical narratology was not that radical. Perhaps, instead of revolution, it was a matter of normal, expectable evolution. Perhaps classical narratology was always already postclassical, in the same way as structuralism is always already post-structuralist and the modern always already post-modern. Perhaps even the most austere and intransigent formalism is not without some openness and flexibility" ("Classical and/or Postclassical" 119).

6. In fact, Liv Hausken challenges exactly this application of the concept of narrator to media like film in her "coda" to Ryan's *Narrative across Media* collection, "Textual Theory and Blind Spots in Media Studies."

this topic more explicitly in her 2006 book *Avatars of Story*. There she provides a particularly clear list of what different media "can easily do," "can do only with difficulty," "cannot do," and instances where a medium "make up for its limitations through these strategies." For example, images can easily immerse the spectator in space, map the storyworld, and represent beauty, but struggle to articulate causal relations and represent things that are not the case or show the flow of time (19–20). Viewed in this way, narrative is a broad quality that various works can have to differing degrees—they "have narrativity" rather than "being a narrative" ("Introduction" 9). This shift has produced a lively subfield of "transmedial narratology" that examines the way that particular media are able to use their degree of narrativity. Recently, Jan-Noël Thon has offered a partial critique and correction to this understanding of transmedial narratology in *Transmedial Narratology and Contemporary Media Culture* (2016). He argues that "a genuinely transmedial narratology is not (or should not be) the same as a collection of medium-specific narratological terms and concepts" (15) and cites *Narrative across Media* as symptomatic, "as the majority of the contributions are concerned with the specific mediality of a single narrative medium" (15). In contrast, Thon's ambitious book examines the way that broad concepts like storyworld, the narrator, and character subjectivity are handled differently by different media, in the process developing a list of strategies that are able to move between individual media—even if they are not fully medium-independent.

As these two examples suggest, digital media has had a prominent place within postclassical narratology. In their 2010 book on postclassical narratology Alber and Fludernik call out new media and "hyperfictions" as exemplary of a transmedial approach that "seeks to rebuild narratology so that it can handle new genres and storytelling practices across a wide spectrum of media" (8). Here digital narrative is one of the many media forms that are available to analysis as our theories become more flexible: "plays, films, narrative poems, conversational storytelling, hyperfictions, cartoons, ballets, video clips, paintings, statues, advertisements, historiography, news stories, narrative representations in medical or legal contexts, and so forth" (9). Along with conversational storytelling and the graphic novel, digital media is often used as a metonym for those narrative forms absent from classical narratology, thus giving these forms a disproportionate share of attention. But unlike these other media, the digital has an undeniable "newness" that makes it particularly attractive to postclassical narratology. When Barthes was writing his pronouncement about the universality of narrative, digital storytelling was not available as a case study. As a result, digital narrative is an enticing object for those narrative theorists who want to examine the relationship between media and the theoretical framework we bring to bear on them.

DIGITAL MEDIA AS NARRATIVE THEORY

That is how the relationship between digital media and narrative theory looks from the point of view of a narrative theorist. How does this history change if we focus, instead, on the history of digital media?

In 1962, a few years before Barthes's essay announcing the universality of narrative, Steve Russell (working with Martin Graetz and Wayne Wiitanen) developed the space combat video game *Spacewar*. This was not the first computer game, but it was the first that looks like a modern game.[7] We tend to think of early computing as focused narrowly on calculation, but in reality applications concerned with language and play were among the first developed.[8] In *Track Changes: A Literary History of Word Processing*, Matthew Kirschenbaum notes that the IBM MT/ST, which was essentially an early word processor that stored keystrokes that could be played back for retyping, was introduced in 1964 but in development since 1956. And, although we often trace the origins of computer games to the popular 1976 text game *Adventure*, experimentation with artificial intelligence and text parsing that is the precondition of this game was occurring throughout this period. In *Twisty Little Passages: An Approach to Interactive Fiction*, Nick Montfort argues that the first text adventure game should be considered not *Adventure* but *SHRDLU*, a dialog-based simulated world consisting of a tabletop with blocks on it, which was developed between 1968 and 1970. In other words, text processing and games were a part of computing from the very beginning, and the exploration of how agent, conflict, dialog—ideas central to if not constitutive of narrative—could be developed using a computer was an active topic of conversation throughout the 60s and 70s.

When we look ahead from this period, Brenda Laurel's 1991 *Computers as Theater* stands out as an exemplary work that articulates a fundamental con-

---

7. In particular, see Rune Klevjer's discussion of the avatar in the video game, which treats the ship in *Spacewar* as consistent with later and more elaborate examples of player characters.

8. For example, Steven Jones has recently told the story of Robert Busa's 1949 work with IBM to develop a concordance to the works of St. Thomas Aquinas using early punch-card machines in *Roberto Busa, S. J., and the Emergence of Humanities Computing: The Priest and the Punched Cards*.

nection between computers and narrative—not just that some digital works can create narratives, but that narrative provides the very structure of the computer itself. She offers this explanation of *Spacewar*:

> Why was *Spacewar* the "natural" thing to build with this new technology? Why not a pie chart or an automated kaleidoscope or a desktop? Its designers identified *action* as the key ingredient and conceived *Spacewar* as a game that could provide a good balance between thinking and doing for its players. They regarded the computer as a machine naturally suited for representing things that you could see, control, and play with. Its interesting potential lay not in its ability to perform calculations but in its capacity to *represent action in which humans could participate.* (1)

Laurel goes on to discuss the computer interface in terms of how it organizes different forms of agency and representation. What is especially interesting here is that the theatrical model is invested in the representation of agency, causality, and event—all fundamental components of narrative.

As we think about the timing of Laurel's book, it is difficult to overstate the influence of Apple's visual metaphors in the original Macintosh (1984) for popularizing the link between the computer interface and our imaginative understanding of metaphorical spaces and agency. In fact, *The Apple Human Interface Guidelines,* first published in 1987, created an extensive commentary on the nature of human–computer interface that is at the heart of Laurel's theater metaphor. Just a year earlier Laurel had edited a collection of essays called *The Art of Human Interface Design* for Apple. In that collection the influential programmer Alan Kay accounts for the origins of his understanding of user interfaces by discussing work on children's learning in the late 1960s (195), before ending with a decidedly narrative explanation of the challenges of user interface metaphors: "At the most basic level the thing we most want to know about an agent is not how powerful it can be, but how trustable it is. In other words, the agent must be able to explain itself well so that we have confidence it will be working on our behalf as a goal sharer rather than as a demented genie recently escaped from *The Arabian Nights*" (206).

All this is to say that right in the middle of the period of classical narratology, when some of the field's defining works were being published, so too was a form of playful computing animated by broadly narrative issues of agency and space in active development. Indeed, the curious similarity of dates is striking: the first widely disseminated computer games, *Adventure* and *Zork,* were developed in 1976 and 1978–79 (respectively), at just the time that works like Chatman's *Story and Discourse* and F. K. Stanzel's *A Theory of Nar-*

rative (1978 and 1979, respectively) were published. Much of this is a matter of coincidence, of course. I will argue in chapter 5 that there is a stronger direct link between possible world theory and computer databases, but there is no reason that *Zork* and the books by Chatman and Stanzel should have aligned so perfectly. But there is an unexpectedly strong overlap between theorizing about narrative and computing during this formative period. Here, for example, is how Russell explained to Stewart Brand why experimenting with a two-dimensional CRT display led him to conclude "that naturally the obvious thing to do was spaceships" for *Spacewar*:

> I had just finished reading "Doc" Smith's *Lensman* series. He was some sort of scientist but he wrote this really dashing brand of science fiction. The details were very good and it had an excellent pace. His heroes had a strong tendency to get pursued by the villain across the galaxy and have to invent their way out of their problem while they were being pursued. That sort of action was the thing that suggested Spacewar. He had some very glowing descriptions of spaceship encounters and space fleet maneuvers. (51)

Obviously, Russell is not framing *Spacewar* as an exploration of technical narrative concepts like free indirect discourse or focalization, but his interest in dynamic displays and interacting objects is informed by a narrative interest in pursuit and antagonism. More broadly, the popularization of computing as a form of storytelling (manifested in a game like *Zork*) occurs at almost the same time that modern narrative theory achieves is classic articulations. In other words, there is already a lot of narrative theory in early experiments in computer design.

Looked at in this way, the digital is not just one of several other media to which narrative theory would turn in order to broaden its models in postclassical theory. Instead, modern narrative theory develops at the same time that digital narrative is emerging, and both seemingly distinct fields share the goal of thinking about the nature of story and meaning. I have treated Marie-Laure Ryan as a theorist of transmedial narratology, but her first book was on digital media, the 1991 *Possible Worlds, Artificial Intelligence, and Narrative Theory*. In rereading her introduction to that book today, I think that she undersells the inevitability of the connection between these two fields. Instead of arguing that digital media is fundamentally intertwined with narrative theory, she chooses to emphasize things like the interdisciplinary nature of the applications of the computer (5) and its literal-mindedness, which "can teach literary critics how to explore and formulate their assumptions" (6). While no doubt true, I would state this link more strongly: since at least 1960, both narrative theorists and computer programmers and designers have been investigating some of the same questions about agent, event, and plot.

Narrative theorists and computer programmers have gone about answering these questions in different ways—the former by offering theoretical models to account for the range of narratives created by other people, and the latter by creating programs that are able to induce in users some sort of feeling of narrative. This can involve the retelling of a beloved novel in game form, such as the influential early text adventure *The Hitchhiker's Guide to the Galaxy* (1984). The overlap of narrative theorizing and computer experimentation is also clear in the dialog of *Eliza* (1964–66), the natural-language processing experiment that did a surprisingly convincing job of imitating the responses of a therapist. In his 1976 book *Computing Power and Human Reason*, Eliza's programmer Joseph Weizenbaum reflects on the lessons of her success: "At bottom, no matter how it may be disguised by technological jargon, the question is whether or not every aspect of human thought is reducible to a logical formalism, or, to put it into the modern idiom, whether or not human thought is entirely computable" (12). This attitude strikes me as typical of the context of the work on modern computing in the 1960s and 70s: that experimental programming inevitably ended up exploring questions of person, consciousness, and knowledge, all topics intimately connected to how we tell stories. As Weizenbaum writes later, "To know with certainty that a person understood what has been said to him is to perceive his entire belief structure and *that* is equivalent to sharing his entire life experience. It is precisely barriers of this kind that artists, especially poets, struggle against" (193).[9]

This broader context of playful computing experimentation helps us to see the better-known examples of computer/narrative fusions in a new light. Let us take the case of the much-discussed Storyspace hypertext system. Developed by Jay David Bolter and Michael Joyce during the mid-1980s and introduced formally in 1987, Storyspace has been a bit of a flash point in debates about the best way to analyze digital texts. Joyce's *afternoon: a story* (1987) provided an almost universal early example of the literary uses of digital media. Stuart Moulthrop's 1992 *Victory Garden* and Shelley Jackson's 1995 *Patchwork Girl* used the system very differently, and explored very different themes. Taken together, these three works provided scholars with a coherent set of example texts that helped to shape the reception of the nascent field of

---

9. The careers of other computer visionaries like Theodor Nelson, J. C. R. Licklider, and Norbert Wiener each provide examples of the broader philosophical context in which early computing emerged. A particularly good example is Douglas Engelbart's interest in Benjamin Lee Whorf on the issue of the way that a computing device might create "associations" and how those are related to "connections" in the human mind. See Thierry Bardini's *Bootstrapping* (40–2) for a discussion of Whorf's influence on Engelbart.

electronic literature. It is precisely the ease with which Storyspace reinforced familiar literary expectations that sparked Espen Aarseth's 1997 critique of the "Storyspace school of hypertext" (85), since for him such works represent a very particular vision of digital media narrowly constrained by its literary context. Elsewhere, Aarseth writes about literary digital works in this way: "These novels are games only in a metaphorical sense; they tease us, but we are not real players. In the case of hypertext fictions, we are explorers but without recognizable rules, there is no real game. To equalize these metaphorical games with a real game is to marginalize an already (academically) marginal phenomenon, to privilege the *illusion* of play over real play" ("Genre" 53).

When Joyce tells the story of creating Storyspace in his essay collection *Of Two Minds,* his framework confirms all of Aarseth's concerns. He recounts his interest in developing this system as a component of his literary life as the publisher of a small-press novel, initially as a tool to aid in the writing and editing of the manuscript. His ambitions shift, though, and he discovers that what he really wants is "to write a novel that would change in successive readings and to make those changing versions according to the connections that I had for some time naturally discovered in the process of writing and that I wanted my readers to share" (31). In other words, the creation of Storyspace is not the result of technology but rather a kind of narrative theorizing, as he thinks about how readers grasp "connections" between one part of the story and another. In pointing out Joyce's literary and narrative theorizing, I am agreeing with Aarseth's critique, but with a small change in emphasis and interpretation. I suggest that this kind of theorizing is everywhere in computing culture of the second half of the twentieth century. We can see it in the fascination with Eliza's faux artificial intelligence and in the design of computing hardware and software itself. In *Mechanisms,* Matthew Kirschenbaum discusses the original IBM patent for the hard drive, which is described as a "book [that] can be read without being opened" (80). Likewise, we can think about the distinctly literary language used in operating system design, including the early Xerox Star's introduction of the "document" as the core of the user's work in 1981, which was popularized by Microsoft in the My Documents folder in Windows.[10] Let me be quick to add, however, that I am not suggesting that the only framework for interpreting digital texts is through such narrative and literary models. Aarseth and other "ludologists" who have worked to celebrate expressive forms that are native to these new technologies—rather

---

10. I discuss the prevalence of such literary metaphors in *Computing as Writing.* See also Anouk Lang's discussion "hybrid practices" that "rarely present an entirely new formation but rather create a meshing of old and new technologies and established and emergent modes of interaction" (4).

than mimicking imitations of the novel—are exactly right in their goals. I merely want to suggest that one of the contexts in which many digital texts were developed reflected an interest in thinking about storytelling. In other words, narrative theory provided part of the background against which even relatively ludological digital media emerged.[11]

In addition to this long-running shared interest in narrative questions of mind and agency, the association of "multimedia" with computing has always made the digital an index of our thinking about the relationship between different media. Early "new media" was often represented as a form of multimedia—a merger of text with sound, image, and video. Indeed, in an early "multimedia encyclopedia" of the 1990s published on CD-ROM, this was quite explicit, as text entries were simply supplemented by audio and (more rarely) video resources. In its first imagining, such works combined older media forms.[12] More broadly, there is an argument to be made that the increasing digitalization of the media that we encounter means that all media are digital on some level.[13] In 1986, Friedrich Kittler suggested that optical fiber networks represented a kind of metamedium: "Once movies and music, phone calls and text reach households via optical fiber cables, the formerly distinct media of television, radio, telephone, and mail converge" (1). Katherine Hayles and Jessica Pressman push the timeline back further into the increasing importance of technology in the nineteenth century:

> With the proliferation of technical media in the latter half of the nineteenth century, that illusion [of writing as 'simple and straightforward'] became much more difficult to sustain, for intervening between writer and reader was a proliferating array of technical devices, including telegraphs, phonographs, typewriters, Dictaphones, Teletypes, and wire recorders, on up to digital computing devices that themselves are splitting into an astonishing array of different protocols, functionalities, interfaces, and codes. (ix)

Focusing on changes just in the last two decades, Lev Manovich has traced the way that medium-specific tools are increasingly being simulated by digital tools—such as the "filter" we might apply to an image. At the outset of

---

11. Although Aarseth is associated with pushing back on the "story fetishism" of early scholarship on digital media ("Genre" 49), his work has always been deeply engaged with narrative theory. See, for example, his discussion of the story/game issue as a "meta-debate" in "A Narrative Theory of Games." See also Astrid Ensslin's discussion of the long-running relationship between literature and play in *Literary Gaming*.

12. I discuss the history of the "multimedia" encyclopedia in *Writing at the Limit*.

13. In "The .txtual Condition" Matthew Kirschenbaum argues that our approach to primary texts must change now that digital forms and metadata are part of our basic composition practices.

Software Takes Command (2013), Manovich asks, "What happens to the idea of a 'medium' after previously media-specific tools have been simulated and extended in software? Is it still meaningful to talk about different mediums at all? Or do we now find ourselves in a new brave world of a single monomedium, or a metamedium? (4). It seems clear that, at least since the *New Grolier Multimedia Encyclopedia* in 1992, digital media has been associated with the friction between one medium and another.

The digital, in other words, has a special relationship to narrative. Sometimes it is treated simply as one among many other media; indeed, this idea is implicit in the ludologists's urging that such media be given the space to develop their own forms and terms. At other times, the digital is treated as a unique moment in the history of media, the point at which previously distinct media merge. The digital seems destined to occupy this quite incoherent place within our culture: both one medium among others, and the medium that encompasses all others. Little surprise, then, that the advent of digital media accelerated theorizing about media in narrative.

MEDIA THEORY

The history that I have outlined above demonstrates that the digital poses unique challenges for narrative theory. The energy surrounding the topic of media in narrative testifies to the importance of this issue, but the vagueness with which digital narrative is placed among other media shows that these complexities have not been fully worked through.

Although a history of media theory in general is beyond the scope of an introduction like this, I think that it is worthwhile to recognize that developing a model for the relationship between media has emerged as a particularly urgent issue in the last several decades. John Johnson, writing about what he calls the "novel of media assemblages" of the later twentieth century, says, "Instead of the separability of media, we now find a generalized 'culture medium,' as Don DeLillo refers to it" (5). This idea that multiple media create some sort of whole is implicit in Marshall McLuhan's 1964 *Understanding Media*. He opens the introduction this way:

> After three thousand years of explosion, by means of fragmentary and mechanical technologies, the Western world is imploding. During the mechanical ages we had extended our bodies in space. Today, after more than a century of electric technology, we have extended our central nervous system itself in a global embrace, abolishing both space and time as far as our planet is concerned. Rapidly, we approach the final phase of the exten-

sions of man—the technological simulation of consciousness, when the creative process of knowing will be collectively and corporately extended to the whole of human society, much as we have already extended our senses and our nerves by the various media. (3–4)

For McLuhan, the rise of "electric technology" creates new media that becomes part of human consciousness itself. McLuhan's work is more suggestive and provocative rather than precise, but this observation that media need to be examined together has had far-reaching and lasting impacts. Writing just a year later in 1965, Dick Higgins coined the term "intermedia" ("an uncharted land that lies between collage, music, and theater" [16]) to describe an experimentalism that disregarded traditional disciplinary boundaries. As I have just suggested, the emergence of digital media has only pushed this intermediality further.

A central challenge, then, has been developing models for how media relate to each other, and how we can historicize the emergence and decline of media over time.[14] Jay David Bolter and Richard Grusin's 1999 *Remediation* is both typical and highly influential, so it deserves some attention here at the outset of this book. They define their central term as "the representation of one medium in another"; the digital uses remediation to position itself against earlier media: "What might seem at first to be an esoteric practice is so widespread that we can identify a spectrum of different ways in which digital media remediate their predecessors, a spectrum depending on the degree of perceived competition or rivalry between the new media and the old" (45). Defined in this way, media constantly jockey for position within their own cultural moment. Bolter and Grusin claim that remediation is a characteristic of digital media. They also suggest that it is a general quality of the relationship between one medium and another:

> It would seem, then, that *all* mediation is remediation. We are not claiming this as an a priori truth, but rather arguing that at this extended historical moment, all current media function as remediators and that remediation offers us a means of interpreting the work of earlier media as well. Our culture conceives of each medium or constellation of media as it responds to, redeploys, competes with, and reforms other media. (55)

The phrasing here is somewhat ambiguous, since this passage suggests that all media history looks like remediation *from our current moment,* without

---

14. This is a departure from older media theories, such as the abstraction and formalism of Lessing's theory of spatial and temporal arts in *Laocoön*.

suggesting that remediation itself is universal. Still, this ambiguity suggests how vexed this issue of the relation between our current moment and media history is.

What is especially important about Bolter and Grusin's book is that it clearly brings together two questions about media: how do media relate to each other, and how do we account for the history of media? What *Remediation* accomplishes, in fact, is making these two questions the same: media compete with each other synchronically, we can say, in exactly the same way that they compete diachronically. In both cases, a medium seeks to discredit or render irrelevant an already established medium to demonstrate that the newer medium can do everything that the earlier medium does, but better. As they write, "The goal of remediation is to refashion or rehabilitate other media" (56). We might take as a simple comparison the way that Netflix's streaming service reforms the older format of the DVD. While both allow the display of video content, Netflix allows users to "watch instantly" without planning ahead (buying or borrowing disks), allows users to rate the video and receive other suggestions, and makes possible the instant jump to similar content. Netflix here promises to remediate the limitations of the older DVD format, while accomplishing everything that older medium can.

Bolter and Grusin's implicit argument that an account of media relations is also an account of media history is the dominant paradigm for contemporary media theory. One popular way of talking about media relations is as an "ecology." Although this model is often imprecise and means different things to different scholars, Ursula Heise describes it as implying three features: "the way in which such technologies form a cultural environment that most of its inhabitants take for granted, but that nevertheless shapes their cognitive possibilities and social behavior in significant ways; second, the ways in which changes in one individual technology change the media configuration and its manner of operation as a whole; and third, the ways in which such technologies function as systems with a logic of their own" (157). As in Bolter and Grusin's theory, here an account of the relationship between media and their constitutive roles is also a way to explain how media change. Both remediation and ecology models put dynamic relations at the center of an account of media.

The media history that I am trying to tell in this book does not accord well with this model, however. Consider, for example, Brenda Laurel's description of computing cited above: "Its interesting potential lay not in its ability to perform calculations but in its capacity to *represent action in which humans could participate.*" Laurel's emphasis here is less on the newness of this medium or its competition with others than on the way that we think about the representation of action in general. This is why she immediately turns to the theater to consider the nature of that representational space. In other words, digital media prompts her to think about core theoretical ideas, such as what it means to represent action. The way that she turns to older media with new eyes tells us rather a lot about how digital narrative will perform its theoretical work. It is, we will see, a model for reconsideration rather than innovation for its own sake. In other words, digital texts tend not to ask implicitly "What kinds of new stories can we create?" or "How can we evoke new kinds of characters?"—the sorts of inquiries that we would expect if we assume that technology is a matter of progress and remediation. Instead, we will see that digital narrative is more likely to implicitly ask, "What is a plot anyway?" or "What does it mean to explore a world?" In other words, I will investigate how digital narrative interrogates our narrative concepts rather than how it pursues new kinds of stories.

The central role of historical reconsideration and rewriting makes the recent work on "media archaeology" particularly relevant in this book. Although it is easy to identify the common concerns and goals of media archaeology, it is a field that does not have precise boundaries. As Jussi Parikka notes in *What Is Media Archaeology?*, "The amount of work that is in spirit even if not always explicitly in name, media-archaeological is vast" (14). The strongest unifying theme in media archaeology is a resistance to the teleological inclination of so much work on technology. Looking back, the emergence of technologies like photography or film can seem almost inevitable, as if human society was simply waiting for the component science and manufacturing to be able to create the conditions for these media forms. In *Reading Writing Interfaces,* Lori Emerson describes her goal as uncovering "a nonlinear and nonteleological series of media phenomena—or ruptures—as a way to avoid reinstating a model of media history that tends towards narratives of progress and generally ignores neglected, failed, or dead media" (xiii). Viewed in this way, we can also include work that discusses what Charles Acland calls "residual media," "the fact that things and practices hang around long past their supposed use-by date" (xvi). Media archaeology also looks to complicate the notion of beginnings—breaking with a simple model of a founding moment. As Wolfgang Ernst remarks in the collection *Media Archaeology,* "Archaeology of media is not simply an alternative form of reconstructing beginnings of media on the macrohistorical scale; instead, it describes technological 'beginnings' of operativity on the microtechnological level" (240). A corollary to this resistance to teleology is a suspicion towards the priority given to the new. An emphasis on the *new* obviously creates an expectation of inevitable progress, and that expectation in turn predisposes us towards a particular way of thinking about the future. Sarah Kember and Joanna Zylinska note, "Questions about future media and about the future of the media [. . .] are part and parcel of the debates about the 'newness' of media" (5). To inquire into the technologies that have lingered on, or that have appeared momentarily and then died a quick death, is to think about other possible futures. As Parikka explains, "Media archaeology has been interested in excavating the past in order to understand the present and future" (2). In focusing on overlooked historical moments, media archaeology shares with new historicism a fascination with the anecdotal and seemingly trivial, and celebrates the variant (Emerson xiii).[15]

One component of this critique of teleology is an emphasis on individual human actors and their contingent choices. Lisa Gitelman is particularly relevant when offering a critique of *Remediation*, which has "a tendency to treat media as the self-acting agents of their own history" (9). A new medium is taken to "remediate" an older medium without ever quite accounting for the individual human agents involved in making these shifts. The alternative temptation is to associate agency with a single visionary inventory—Gitelman's example is Friedrich Kittler's discussion of Edison—without recognizing the complexity of any moment when an invention is supposed to have occurred. In general, media archaeology treats the history of media not as some all-encompassing system in which changes propagate through the whole environment impersonally. Instead, it looks for individual decision points and the alternatives that go unexplored and remain latent.

This summary should make clear that my inquiry into digital media's relationship to narrative theory is not directly a project on media archaeology. My interest is primarily the scope and development of our conceptual models and terms for narrative, rather than the particular physical devices through which narratives might be produced. What I want to draw from media archaeology is a nuanced sense of history that recognizes the interaction between technology and the cultural frameworks that we bring to bear upon it. In particular, I am interested in this archaeology's tendency to read backwards rather than forwards as a way to resist technological teleology. What are the conditions within the theoretical landscape that can make possible a response to technical developments and changes? In the account that I will offer in this book, digital media does not itself so much create new forms of narrative as exploit tensions that already exist within core narrative concepts. I will describe a development of narrative through digital media that takes advantage of ambiguities or questions left unanswered—and often unasked—in theory based on the novel. Hayles offers something of the same attitude in *My Mother Was a Computer*, where

---

15. Erkii Huhtamo and Jussi Parikka briefly discuss the similarities between media ecology and new historicism in their introduction to *Media Archaeology: Approaches, Applications, and Implications*, although it would be "too gross a generalization" to say that "media archaeology is new historicist in its essence" (2).

she writes, "These changed senses of work, text, and document make it possible to see phenomena that are now obscured or made invisible by the reigning ideologies" (105). My assumption here is that what makes individual uses of narrative in digital media seem compelling is not so much how they break from the past, but how they make use of established forms in ways that expose faulty assumptions or incomplete elements of our core narrative concepts.

METHOD AND DEFINITIONS

Each of the chapters that makes up this book focuses on one common narrative concept: narrator, setting, event, character, and world. In each case, I argue that digital media allows us to see complexity and unexplored potential in common narrative concepts: the game designer that is not quite the implied author or narrator, the orienting space that is more than simply the setting for the story, the way that character and movement are intertwined. These narrative "innovations" are not so much a matter of discovering some technological ability for narrative. Instead, digital media simply provides a context in which these possibilities become more obvious. Over the course of this book, we will see that one of the most important ways that digital media helps us to rethink narrative is by emphasizing the physical artifact with which we interact. We have grown so accustomed to the form of the book that we rarely think about our physical interactions with it, and the variety of ways in which it is put to use. Through the central importance of the user interface, digital narrative draws our attention back to all of the ways that we have to engage with and use a narrative. I have kept the structure for this book relatively simple because my goal is to allow complexity to emerge out of these common narrative terms once they are examined through the lens of digital media. From a certain point of view, my organizing terms—setting, narration, character, event, and world—can be seen as somewhat arbitrary. It is precisely the fact that these are such common terms, given to so many practical uses and theoretical articulations, that allows them to serve as our entrance into the tensions and ambiguities of narrative theory as a whole.

As for my sample texts, I have taken a broad approach to defining what I mean by digital narrative, and have intentionally mixed works most commonly categorized as electronic literature with commercial video games and other forms of digital textuality that are not explicitly designed to create narrative experiences. This is not, thus, a book on electronic literature specifically, since my framework is both narrower and broader in different ways. It is narrower because I am excluding many works that have literary significance but are not primarily narrative, like Jim Andrews's reworking of the arcade game *Asteroids* as a game of shooting letters in *Arteroids* (2006). It is broader because I am also interested in digital narrative that has few literary aspirations, and in some cases little textuality itself—such as 3D video games. In framing the project in this way, I am adopting a simple if not unproblematic understanding of the digital.[16] In *My Mother Was a Computer,* Hayles asserts, "With the exception of a handful of fine letterpress books, every book produced in the United States and Europe this year will have been an electronic document in at least one and probably many stages of its existence. Given present modes of book production, it is more accurate to view print as a particular form of output for electronic text than it is to regard print as a realm separate from digital media" (117). In this particular chapter she discusses Neal Stephenson's *Cryptonomicon* as "a work that remains in print but nevertheless bears within its body marks of its electronic composition" (117). In framing the digital's relationship to print, Hayles raises the same issue that I noted in Manovich as well: that as more and more of our creative activity is performed using software, medium becomes more of an effect. This shift can, of course, have a broad impact on how we compose, disseminate, and consume writing—but that impact is more general and diffuse than I want to address in this book.

In this book I have focused on digital works that involve some visible and explicit role for computing, most often in their operation and reception but occasionally in their production. My assumption is that because the digital complicates our access to and interaction with the work it makes us aware of different possibilities for constructing narrative. There are some partial exceptions, but in general I am interested in those digital works whose interface and use the reader must come to understand. This issue of our awareness of the interface is a topic of debate within recent media theory. Lisa Gitelman argues that media go through a cycle of new self-consciousness and familiar transparency:

> Inventing, promoting, and using the first telephones involved lots of self-conscious attention to telephony. But today, people converse through the phone without giving it a moment's thought. [. . .] When one uses antique media like stereoscopes, when one encounters unfamiliar protocols, like

---

16. The boundaries of "electronic literature" are very much a matter of debate. I am following Roberto Simanowski: "If the piece still requires reading as a central activity, we may call it digital literature" (17). This is in contrast to Katherine Hayles, who offers a much broader definition as those works that "interrogate the histories, contexts, and productions of literature, as well as the verbal art of literature proper" (*Electronic Literature* 4). See also Jessica Pressman's argument that such electronic literature, especially "web-based work [. . .] published on or after 2000" involves a "commitment to literariness and a literary past" (*Digital Modernism* 2).

using a pay telephone abroad, or when media break down, like the Hubble Space Telescope, forgotten questions about whether and how media do the job can bubble to the surface. (5–6)

She concludes, "When media are new, they offer a look into the different ways that their jobs get constructed as such" (6). Of course, this is not a permanent condition. Lori Emerson observes that contemporary computing strives towards making the interface disappear: "What is new is that the interfaces themselves and therefore their constraints are becoming ever more difficult to perceive" (ix). She has in mind wearable devices like Google Glass and the simplified interface of the iPad, but I think that the point that she raises applies to digital technology in general. Gitelman would likely agree that these devices—certainly the iPad more than Google Glass—represent a certain way that the digital is designed to make protocols clear and simple for average users. Even in these cases, such receding interfaces give us a chance to think about the uses that they enable. In this book, I emphasize digital works that evoke familiar narrative expectations and goals using elements of the digital medium that depart from what was possible in print or film. Indeed, it is precisely this combination of the familiar and the new that makes these works particularly productive sites for examining narrative concepts.

At the outset of this project it is worthwhile to acknowledge that the question of "newness" in art is a relatively undertheorized concept, but one that is an inevitable issue in the work of these digital narratives. Although it is not my goal to offer a general theory of newness, I would like to sketch an outline of my assumptions on this topic, since they inform the analysis that is to come. As we have seen, the problem of newness is central to the way that media archeology seeks to complicate our traditional ways of thinking about progress. Writing back in 1975, Hayden White tried to address "The Problem of Change in Literary History" and provides a helpful orientation on this topic. White frames the question in an admirably broad way:

> Such an analysis would not commit us to a crudely reductive or monocausal conceptualization of the field. We would not necessarily be forced to say that one of the elements in the field, such as the historical context, the audience, the artist, or the work, enjoys the status of a supreme causal agency of which the other elements are effects or secondary manifestations. In all probability, in fact, we should be forced to conclude that different elements play different roles as agents, agencies, and effects at different times and places in the historical continuum. (98)

White goes on to note that any historical account will choose a level of generality to address—from the individual details of particular literary works, all the way up to the claims about the whole historical context. An observation that White makes in this account strikes me as potentially powerful in helping us to integrate an interest in change and a greater appreciation of the work of individual writers and artists in that process. He is worth quoting at some length:

> In a given period and place in history the system of encodation and decodation permits the transmission of certain *kinds of messages regarding the context* and not others; and it will favor those genres adequate to the establishment of contacts between different points in the whole communication system represented by language in general. *Significant periods of literary change* will thus be signaled by *changes in the linguistic code*; changes in the code will in turn be reflected in changes in both the cognitive content of literary works (the messages) and the codes of contact (genres) in which messages are transmitted and received. Changes in the code, finally, can be conceived to be reflective of changes in the historiconatural context in which a given language game is being played. Writers may experiment with different genres, with different messages, even with different systems of encodation and decodation. But a given product of such experimentation will find an audience "programmed" to receive innovative messages and contacts only if the sociocultural context is such as to sustain an audience whose experience of that context corresponds to the *modes of message formulation and conveyance* adopted by a given writer. (107–8)

Although very broad, White frames this question in a helpful way by suggesting that we can view literary change as the result of shifts in the conditions of possible activity by writers and other artists. Obviously, these shifts can take many forms: from changing ideas about who can be a writer, what the appropriate subject matter for a poem is, the physical form that a book must take, and so forth. What strikes me as especially interesting about White's claim is that it encourages us to focus on the preconditions for change. As White suggests, new literary work will arise when an audience is able to "receive innovative messages," and we might think of this receptivity in terms of the continuities between existing and new literary forms.[17]

---

17. For a different approach to newness grounded in Deleuze, see Audrey Wasser's recent *The Work of Difference*, which examines the romantic and modernist understanding of newness. See also Laura Marcus's discussion of cinema in "How Newness Enters the World."

In each of the chapters I will show that digital media draws on existing narrative concepts—narration, setting, character, event, and world—and innovates by exploring limitations or ambiguities in the way that these concepts have been deployed in other media. To use White's language, the audience for digital narrative has been "programmed" to recognize new forms of digital narrative because those forms depend on reconfiguring possibilities that are implicit but undeveloped in these other media. This is a break from the way that we have tended to talk about technology and storytelling, which has emphasized the ways that the new medium allows artists to do things that were impossible in the past. The approach that I am describing here focuses on the way that the field is constructed to enable certain kinds of innovations to be adopted using the new technology. In particular, I will show that that this field contains blind spots and ambiguities that digital media have been able to take advantage of in constructing "new" kinds of narrative.

Interest in the preconditions to the new is a central feature of Michael McKeon's *The Origins of the English Novel*. In *The Rise of the Novel*, Ian Watt notes the problem of explaining this origin without appealing to either genius or accident, "the twin faces on the Janus of the dead ends of literary history" (9). We can see McKeon's book as a response to this problem. McKeon summarizes Watt's difficulty as requiring "a theory not just of the rise of the novel but of how categories, whether 'literary' or 'social,' exist in history: how they first coalesce by being understood in terms of—and as transformations of—other forms that have thus far been taken to define the field of possibility" (4). For him, the challenge of describing the "origins of the English novel" is accounting for the fact that there is so much activity before this origin that seems novel-like. For him, what we refer to as this "origin" is really simply a moment at which the "novel" emerges as a valid term to account for all of these various activities: "The origins of the English novel occur at the end point of a long history of 'novelistic usage'—at the moment when this usage has become sufficiently complex to permit a generalizing 'indifference' to the specificity of usages and an abstraction of the category whose integrity is presupposed by that indifference" (19). The novel, in other words, depends on this kind of prehistory that makes it possible. He describes his "procedure in this study [to] be to work back from that point of origin to disclose the immediate history of its 'pre-givenness'" (19).

The origins of digital narrative are not as complex as those of the novel.[18] Nonetheless, I do think that McKeon has something to teach us about the

---

18. There has been a lot of debate about the disciplinary and institutional home for digital media—should it be seen as a literary form or should it be treated primarily in terms of play

preconditions that make something seemingly new possible. I will show that there are practices in the pre-digital use and conceptualization of core narrative qualities that make their new digital forms possible. For McKeon, this process is ultimately a simplification: novelistic practices reach a point at which they can be grouped under the abstract term "the novel" without concern for their individual variations. In the case of digital narrative, the situation is different because practice is more entwined with theory. For McKeon, practice precedes the abstract name "the novel." In the case of digital narrative, our theoretical concepts are more deeply entwined with practice. It is clear that digital artists have a sense that they are updating the idea of "character" or "setting" when they construct these works; consequently, these narrative concepts are the very things that are "pre-given"—to use McKeon's term. In other words, Joseph Weizenbaum may not have been reading narrative theory when he developed Eliza, but he was certainly aware that he was exploring how to create a believable "person" entirely through dialog. Those pre-given concepts are complex—marked by tensions, indeterminacies, and sometimes outright contradictions—but they are what allow seemingly new practices in digital narrative.

This is not to argue that digital artists need necessarily be consciously analyzing these contradictions in order to use them to account for change. We might recall Pierre Bourdieu's claim that the habitus, "internalized as a second nature and so forgotten as history" is "what gives practices their relative autonomy with respect to external determinations of the immediate present" (56). For Bourdieu, the subtle influence of the habitus as "systems of durable, transposable dispositions" (53) is exactly what makes spontaneity possible: "The *habitus* is a spontaneity without consciousness or will, opposed as much to the mechanical necessity of things without history in mechanistic theories as it is to the reflective freedom of subjects 'without inertia' in rationalist theories" (*Logic* 6). In fact, in *The Rules of Art*, Bourdieu describes artistic change and revolution (in this case, focusing on music) in terms quite similar to those that I have repurposed from McKeon. He describes "the revolutionary work of Schoenberg, Berg and Webern as the outcome of a new realization and a systematic [. . .] application of the principles inscribed in an implicit state in the whole musical tradition, a tradition still present in its entirety in works which surpass it by achieving it on another plane" (241–2). I will demonstrate some-

---

and game? And digital media raises issues of archiving that are uniquely complex, since in many cases the hardware for which these texts are designed may not longer be available and are certainly not uniform in the way that library book catalogues are. But these debates are possible precisely because there are institutions in place that can fight over digital media's home and define the difficulty of cataloging and archiving. The early novel had no such competing institutional homes.

thing similar in this book in the way that digital media often offers a "new realization" of forms and concepts that depend on the current structure of the "implicit state" of narrative theory and practice. Obviously, this account may apply more broadly to other forms of innovation—changes in genre, market, and of course other media—but the unique complexity of the theory/practice relationship in digital narrative qualifies any application we might make to other media. This reconsideration of core theoretical terms is likely to be more powerful especially in the case of the migration into a new medium than it is in other historical shifts. More importantly, as I will show, there has been a long-standing theoretical interest in narrative among practitioners in digital media that makes the role of theoretical reconsideration particularly central to creating stories in this medium. From its very beginnings, digital narrative is also narrative theory.

CHAPTER 1

Narration, Intrigue, and Reader Positioning in Digital Narrative

IT MIGHT seem tautological to say that the process of narration is central to narrative. James Phelan has summarized narrative concisely as "somebody telling somebody else on some occasion and for some purpose(s) that something happened" (*Living* 18). But narration has not always been the focus of narrative theory. Writing in 1979, F. K. Stanzel argued for "mediacy of presentation as the generic characteristic of narration" (4). In framing narrative in this way, Stanzel is implicitly breaking with the structuralist methodology that had dominated the previous decade, whose emphasis on narrative syntax and morphology had de-emphasized the act of storytelling. Ross Chambers put this somewhat more broadly in 1984: "With the waning of structuralism, it has become clear that, in general terms, meaning is not inherent in discourse and its structures but contextual, a function of the pragmatic situation in which the discourse occurs" (3).

The central role of narration in the study of narrative over the last three decades has produced a lively discussion of the entities presumably responsible for this act of telling someone that something has happened. In *Story and Discourse*, Seymour Chatman summarizes:

> Narratives are communications, thus easily envisaged as the movement of arrows from left to right, from author to audience. But we must distinguish between real and implied authors and audiences: only implied authors and

audiences are immanent to the work, constructs of the narrative-transaction-as-text. The real author and audience of course communicate, but only through their implied counterparts. (31)

Whether any narrative can ever be attributed to a real author unmediated by the implied author, and whether a narrator is necessary to other media like film has been the subject of endless debates.

Given the importance of narration and the intense interest in digital narrative, it is surprising indeed that little attention has been given to the way that it is deployed in electronic texts. An important exception to this is Espen Aarseth's discussion of "cybertext" narration in his landmark *Cybertext* (1997). Aarseth's discussion arises out of his analysis of the text adventure game, in which he coined the term *intrigue* to refer to "a sequence of oscillating activities effectuated (but certainly not controlled) by the user" (112). That is, intrigue describes those actions that a user must perform in order to move the game forward. Aarseth's use of this term is quite narrow: he sees it as a feature that is specific to the games that he examines and that replaces the structure of narration that is central to traditional storytelling. In this chapter, I will argue for the broader applicability of Aarseth's concept of intrigue. Specifically, I will show that intrigue is a structure implicit in almost all electronic narratives and that it complements rather than replaces the narration *also* found in these texts. In other words, I will argue that these stories have both narration and intrigue, both narrators and intrigants, narratees and intriguees. In turn, intrigue will provide a model for the chapters that follow by offering a term that applies to other media as well, and that draws attention to the functioning of the story as an object with various uses.

IMPLIED AUTHORS, NARRATORS, AND READERS

A fundamental part of our experience of narrative is extrapolating from the events, settings, and characters described directly to project both the larger story and the moral, philosophical, and social values that define the world in which that story takes place. As Porter Abbott puts it,

> We are always called upon to be active participants in narrative, because receiving the story depends on how we in turn construct it from the discourse. Are stories, then, at the mercy of the reader and how diligently he or she reads? To a certain degree this is true. But most stories, if they succeed—that is, if they enjoy an audience or readership—do so because they

have to some extent successfully controlled the process of story construction. (*Cambridge* 21–2)

From the beginning of modern narrative theory, critics have recognized that this control means that readers intuit the values they are expected to hold. Iser describes our responsibilities as the "implied reader" this way: "He [the implied reader] embodies all those predispositions necessary for a literary work to exercise its effect—predispositions laid down, not by an empirical outside reality, but by the text itself" (34). Discovering these predispositions and using them to interpret the meaning of the work involves a circular process that James Phelan calls a "feedback loop": "The author designs the textual phenomena for a hypothetical audience [. . .], and the individual rhetorical reader seeks to become part of that audience" (*Reading* 18, 19).

Several theoretical entities, which in turn imply "reception positions that interpreters of narrative must regularly—and simultaneously—occupy" (Herman, *Story Logic* 335), are widely accepted as part of current narrative theory. In *Story and Discourse* Seymour Chatman helped to codify our understanding of the various entities involved in narration by distinguishing among the real author, the implied author, the narrator, the narratee, the implied reader, and the real reader (147). At the same time, Peter Rabinowitz's subtle distinction between the authorial and narrative audience achieved widespread acceptance and refined understandings of the idea of the implied reader. Rabinowitz explains:

> Every author designs his or her work rhetorically for a specific hypothetical audience. But since a novel is generally an imitation of some nonfictional form (usually history, including biography and autobiography), the narrator of the novel (implicit or explicit) is generally an imitation of an author. He or she writes for an *imitation* audience (which I call the *narrative audience*) that also possesses particular knowledge. The narrator of *War and Peace* appears to be a historian. As such, he is writing for an audience that not only knows (as does the authorial audience) that Moscow was burning in 1812, but that also believes that Natasha, Pierre, and Andrei "really" existed, and that the events in their lives "really" took place. (94–5)

Phelan provides a nice example of the distinction between authorial and narrative audiences: in Browning's "My Last Duchess," the narrative audience ignores the rhymes and meter of the poem and treats the Duke as a realistic dramatic speaker, while the authorial audience is aware of the artificial elements of the poem's formal design (*Reading People* 5).

There has been some pushback against the proliferation of these theoretical entities. Writing in 1997 Richard Walsh offered a particularly provocative critique of insisting on imposing such layers to narration universally. He focuses on Gerard Genette's distinction between extradiegetic heterodiegetic and homodiegetic narrators—that is, between "a narrator [. . .] who tells a story he is absent from" and "a narrator [. . .] who tells his own story" after the narrative events have been completed (*Narrative Discourse* 248). For Walsh, giving special status to a narrator as somehow ontologically different from the characters of the story is unnecessary:

> My argument against the narrator, then, comes down to this: Fictions are narrated by their authors, or by characters. Extradiegetic homodiegetic narrators, being represented, are characters, just as all intradiegetic narrators are. Extradiegetic heterodiegetic narrators (that is, "impersonal" and "authorial" narrators), who cannot be represented without thereby being rendered homodiegetic or intradiegetic, are in no way distinguishable from authors. (510–11)

Likewise, there has been an extensive debate about the degree to which the implied author "exists." Patrick Colm Hogan provides a helpful summary of the debate about how closely the implied author is tied to a person:

> If one opts for "tied to a person," then one faces the further problem of distinguishing the implied author from the real author. Some writers, such as James Phelan, see the implied author as a "streamlined version of the real author, an actual or purported subset of the real author's capacities, traits, attitudes, beliefs, values, and other properties." Other writers see the implied author as an idealized version of the real author. (23; citing Phelan, *Living* 45)

This critique is related to work that gives new attention to omniscient narration, seen since the modernists as old-fashioned and unsophisticated, as an overlooked element of literary history. Paul Dawson explains the irony particularly well in his discussion of contemporary literature:

> By the mid-twentieth century, when the modernist ideal of effacing the textual presence of the author, of a retreat from overt opinion into the interior lives of characters, became entrenched as an aesthetic principle, it was buttressed by both the "intentional fallacy" of the New Criticism, and the fundamental narratological distinction between an author and narrator. In other words, the meaning and structure of a work could be separated from

consideration of authorial intent. Yet at the same time, the presence of the author in the public sphere became increasingly important to the marketing of fiction. (13)

Dawson goes on to argue that some contemporary authors rhetorically use their image as an author to play the role of a public intellectual: "Contemporary omniscient narration is an overt attempt to parlay the conventional authority of a fictional narrator into cultural authority for the author" (21).

Despite these debates, most recent narrative theory has taken a relatively pragmatic approach to these hypothetical entities, and focused on their explanatory power. Hogan wraps up his review of the implied author debate by emphasizing the "greater explanatory rigor" of treating the implied author as a norm imposed on the reader by the text (35). Or, as Seymour Chatman claims, "My defense is strictly pragmatic, not ontological: the question is not whether the implied author *exists* but what we *get* from positing such a concept"[1] (*Coming to Terms* 75). Indeed, the concept of the implied author may be most valuable where it is most artificial. As Chatman notes, "Films churned out by Hollywood, are made by a consortium of writers, producers, actors, directors, cinematographers [. . .]" but "*seem* to have been created by a single author" (82). Although there remains a lively debate about the scope and value of some of these distinctions, these entities have been broadly accepted as constituting discursive positions with which the reader can identify.

(RE)INTRODUCING INTRIGUE

The issue of how well these positions apply beyond the print text is a particularly complex one. I have already noted the debate between Chatman and Bordwell on whether there is a narrator in film, and of course this is an even more fraught topic as we move into media like painting. The concept of the implied author seems straightforward enough, and Hogan has argued that it is particularly valuable in film and painting, where it helps to construct a unifying "auteur" behind individual works. Whether we can meaningfully talk about a narrator or narratee in painting—even explicitly narrative painting— is a much more problematic issue.

---

1. As with other chapters, any emphasis in quotes is from the original text, unless otherwise noted.

Digital media would initially seem to be a less challenging case for narration, since textuality is so common a feature of this work. Even in cases of largely visual video games, explicit voice-over narration is quite common. In fact, I would like to start by considering the case of a small electronic feature that merely modifies a primarily textual structure: the hyperlink. In *Avatars of Story*, Marie-Laure Ryan reviews the hyperlink typologies of previous critics and synthesizes them into a six-part model. *Temporal* links jump us forward or backward in the story. *Simultaneity* links move us to another set of actions going on at the same time. *Perspective switching* links jump to a different focalization of the story. *Digressive* or background links give us information that explains what is going on in the present of the story. *Choose-your-own-adventure* links ask the reader to make a decision about how the characters should act in the story. Ryan refers to a sixth link type as *spatial*, by which she means not the jump to another literal place in the story, but instead the shift to another section of text, or lexia, linked through theme and imagery. Although these hyperlinks remind us of transitions in a print narrative, they often cannot clearly be associated with the narrator of an individual lexia. For example, in Caitlin Fisher's *These Waves of Girls*, hyperlinks allow the reader to jump to other parts of the story that mention similar characters or topics. For example, the "kissing2" lexia reads,

> Vanessa had always roamed shopping malls alone; quarries. Secretly I harbored large fears in her adultless world, though not in my own sweet terrain where I could run faster, confidently, could wrestle and hold and there was no child who could beat me, not older, not younger, not even my uncle's friends, boys in their teens who I would set upon like a feral child and they would hold back because I was a child and because they were weak.

It is not clear that the speaker is aware of these links, and we must suspect that they are the work of some other agent who has constructed the text.

The reader's ability to become the "implied reader" of such narratives depends on recognizing not just the intentions of the narrators, then, but also how these links have been constructed—what Jeff Parker describes as a "linking schema" or "linkage." But the importance of grasping a text's underlying design applies to more than just hyperlinks. Ryan notes that the user of a computer program "needs a scenario that casts him in a role and projects his actions as the performance of concrete, familiar tasks" (217); she describes different scenarios that the reader might imagine (the text as theater, the text as a space, the text as a supermarket, the text as a kaleidoscope), and concludes, "which one of these scenarios will be preferred depends as much on the individual dispositions of the reader as on the nature of the text" (223). In focusing on the video game, Jesper Juul is more specific about how players grasp the design and rules of a game: "To play a video game is therefore to interact with real rules while imagining a fictional world, and a video game is a set of rules as well as a fictional world" (1). When we play a video game, we have to understand the nature of the fictional world (the places, characters, and events that give the gameworld its shape and coherence), and yet at the same time grasp the rules by which we interact with the game itself. We intuitively understand that in some games our main activity is shooting things, while in others much of our progress is made by navigating spaces, gathering resources, or talking to characters.

For Juul, good game design means consistency between the rules of the game and the shape of the world:

> While the *design* of a game can work by choosing a domain or fictional setting and then subjectively designing rules to implement that domain, the player of a video game experiences this in an inverted way, where the representation and fictional world presented by the game cue the player into making assumptions about the rules of the game. In a computerized soccer game, the fictional world of the game will cue the player to assume that the game implements whatever concept the player has of soccer, including the normal soccer rules. (176)

Although these rules are obviously central to playing a video game, I believe that they apply more broadly to all forms of textuality that require the user to *act,* including hypertext narratives; after all, we must come to understand how the links function before we can grasp the structure of the work and explore it systematically. The importance of the design of electronic narratives and the reader's need to understand their rules make such narratives fundamentally different from traditional print stories. Of course, readers do need to follow rules to move through a printed book: if we did not know that we were supposed to turn the pages to progress through the story, and that each page was supposed to be read according to its numerical order, we would be unable to grasp the meaning of the text. But print has fewer rules for use, and those rules are so broadly adopted that readers usually do not need to think about how they are to be implemented. Electronic texts, conversely, require us to grasp their rules for use on a case-by-case basis.

We are going to see something similar happen in each of the chapters of this book, and in regard to different core narrative concepts. In the case of narration, the digital text draws our attention to something that is generally unappreciated but nonetheless present in other media such as print or film, and that prompts us to return to narrative theory and consider whether our terms and models have been too limited. A central question, at this point, is where these rules fit within conventional narratological accounts of reader positioning. It might seem obvious that the analyst needs to treat these rules as simply another kind of knowledge that readers use in their role as the "authorial audience," but for his part Rabinowitz gives almost no attention to the reader's interaction with the physical artifact of the book. Does the authorial audience know the page number? Does it know what kind of paper the book has been printed upon, or the font that has been chosen? In general, critics have tended to emphasize higher-level issues related to the construction of the story as a discursive rather than physical object. Thus, when Rabinowitz introduces the concept of the authorial audience, his focus is on readers' knowledge about history and genre. Although he assures us that "the potential range of assumptions an author can make [. . .] is infinite" (22), his examples are drawn from a fairly conventional understanding of background knowledge such as historical facts (the Kennedy assassination), cultural references (a tabouleh and pita sandwich), specific books (Hamlet), and genre conventions (the least likely suspect usually turns out to be the murderer in a mystery) (21–2, 39). Likewise, Phelan's analysis of *The French Lieutenant's Woman*, whose metafictional elements would seem to draw attention to the physical artifact of the book, focuses mostly on generic expectations: "This audience, which knows the conventions of both nineteenth- and twentieth-century narration, recognizes the twentieth-century novelist adopting the nineteenth-century conventions and wonders why" (*Reading* 86). Those elements of the work that Phelan associates with the authorial audience—genre, theme, convention—are associated with the unfolding of the story rather than the material properties of the book considered as an artifact in its own right. By contrast, consider the question asked before any of the short, flash narratives on Webyarns.com start: "Is Your Computer's Sound On?" This question addresses the status of the electronic work as a technical artifact and not just the purveyor of a story, implying an awareness of the physical text that differs from the kinds of awareness or knowledge attributed to the authorial audience in most of Rabinowitz's and Phelan's examples.

There is also a more subtle assumption that runs through Rabinowitz's definition of the authorial audience that works against any attempt to take into account material properties of the physical book. In general, in becoming members of the authorial audience readers are embracing an idealized understanding of textual origin and relevant context. Initially, this assertion might seem counterintuitive, since Rabinowitz contrasts the authorial audience and the narrative audience by stressing the authorial audience's greater knowledge about the context of acts of narration—e.g., those performed by character narrators. At the same time, however, the whole point of the authorial audience as a concept is to describe the interpretive moves that the author of a given work expects readers to make and to show how the author is able to control the story's reception. In fact, Rabinowitz notes that entering the authorial audience for a narrative may involve pretending *not* to know something: "Sometimes actual readers can respond to a text as authorial audience only by *not* knowing something that they in fact know—not knowing, as they read John Steinbeck's *In Dubious Battle,* the actual (often unidealistic) course that the American labor movement would eventually follow; not knowing, as they read *U. S. A.,* that Dos Passos would later shift his political views" (33). Arguably, in the terms afforded by Rabinowitz's model, the details of the physical book would normally fall into the category of things that the authorial audience is supposed not to know—or at least not to concern itself with. Authors, in Rabinowitz's account, assume that readers will *not* focus on typefaces or page numbers, unless they are specifically cued to engage with these specifics of the material text.

In this sense, the notion of an authorial audience depends on a concept of authorship that is considerably narrower and culturally more specific than that of the source of a given text in all its material or physical specificity. We would do well to recall Foucault's notion that "the name of an author is not precisely a proper name among others" (*Language* 122). Instead, assigning a piece of writing to an author makes possible certain forms of discursive activity: "In this sense, the function of an author is to characterize the existence, circulation, and operation of certain discourses within a society" (124). Rabinowitz recognizes this dynamic when he notes the importance of ignoring certain modes of knowledge (or kinds of interests) when reading a narrative as a member of the authorial audience, but I want to recast the issue in slightly different terms. Specifically, reading as a member of the authorial audience, as Rabinowitz characterizes that reading position, means that one does not engage with questions about the material history and production of the physical book itself. Books like Mark Z. Danielewski's *House of Leaves* or Steve Tomasula's *VAS,* which explicitly foreground these sorts of questions through their play with typography and page layouts, appear to be exceptions to this rule. But in typographically playful works like these the narrative audience is made aware of these material elements of the text along with the authorial audience. Such works do not provide the book-material equivalent of the Duke's verse and rhyme—something unnoticed by the narrative audience but recognized by the authorial audience. This is because there is no convention that defines the relevance of material elements of the book in the way that the convention of verse defines the relevance of rhyme, meter, and sound.

The electronic work, then, depends on physical elements of the text that fall outside the scope of the knowledge that we usually attribute to the authorial audience. We might expand the concept of the authorial audience to include this knowledge, but I will show that digital narratives often depend on carrying over those more limited conventions from print. Because we will see that electronic narratives continue to depend on these conventions, I think that a better strategy is to posit a different kind of agent responsible for constructing electronic narratives, and a different role for the reader to fulfill when following the rules of such texts. To explain what we gain by theorizing these new positions, let us take as an example an introductory lexia ("work in progress") from Michael Joyce's *afternoon*:

> Closure is, as in any fiction, a suspect quality, although here it is made manifest. When the story no longer progresses, or when it cycles, or when you tire of the paths, the experience of reading it ends. Even so, there are likely to be more opportunities than you think there are at first. A word which doesn't yield the first time you read a section may take you elsewhere if you choose it when you encounter the section again; and sometimes what seems a loop, like memory, heads off again in another direction.
>
> There is no simple way to say this.

The voice in this passage appears to be less a narrator speaking to a narrative audience, as in other parts of the story, and something closer to Joyce himself addressing the authorial audience directly. The speaking agent refers explicitly to generic expectations about the story and knowledge of conventional reading practices—issues directly related to readers' ability to see themselves as (or rather become) members of the authorial audience, in Rabinowitz's and Phelan's terms. In this sense, the kind of knowledge needed to navigate *afternoon* seems to be included in what the authorial audience is supposed to know.

On closer examination, however, we find that this passage withholds information about navigating this text that the reader needs to grasp, suggesting a mismatch between rhetorical theorists' conception of the authorial audience and the knowledge that readers/users need to have to make sense of the work's overall design. Compare Joyce's explanation of the experience of *afternoon* with J. Yellowlees Douglas's well-known description of reading the novel:

> Since the segment "I call" also refused to default the first time I encountered it, what distinguishes my first and last experiences of this physical cue?

> Why does it prompt me, the first time I come across it, to read the narrative again from the beginning, pursuing different connections, yet prompt me to stop reading the second time? The decision to continue reading after my first encounter with "I call" reflected my awareness that the first reading of *afternoon* visited only 36 places out of a total of 539—leaving the bulk of the narrative places still to be discovered on subsequent readings. (102)

Douglas and Joyce both seem to be focusing on the same phenomena: the experience of reading the narrative and the frustrations readers are likely to encounter. Both writers depend on their implied readers' prior knowledge about *afternoon* and its place in relation to a whole range of conventions connected with narrative and genre. But the tone and style of these two passages are very different. Douglas is considerably more direct and specific about the design of the work and the number of lexias contained in it, the choices that readers make, and how readers are to navigate the work. Looking back on "work in progress," we can now notice a lack of specificity. If Joyce wants to explain how the story works, why *not* tell the reader how many lexias it contains in total? Why not reveal which words on the screen are links? Why depend on vague phrasing like "A word which doesn't yield" and "heads off again in another direction" instead of referring more specifically to guard links and reading options? Likewise, why does this passage make no reference to the mechanics of the reading, and to the fact that the reader can reveal the available linked words by clicking on a book icon below the main screen (see figure 1.1)?

We might think that Joyce wants to keep some of this information hidden (especially the total number of lexias in the work), but understanding most of these user interface elements is fundamental to basic reader competence. Why make no reference to that interface? The answer, I think, is far-reaching in its implications: in this passage, Joyce wants to maintain the illusion of being a storyteller rather than the constructor of the artifact with which the reader is presently interacting. This is why his description is more euphemistic than direct, and why he seems unable to make precise references to the brute facts of the interface. In effect, Joyce distinguishes between author and designer—even though both roles are performed by the real-life person, Michael Joyce.

Narrative theory based on printed stories has not yet developed language for talking about the way that electronic texts guide their users to understand these rules. This kind of reader positioning has been explored in some detail in connection with one genre of electronic narratives: the text adventure game or, as it is more commonly described today, interactive fiction. More than this, I suggest that Espen Aarseth's concept of "intrigue" as a reader/text dynamic,

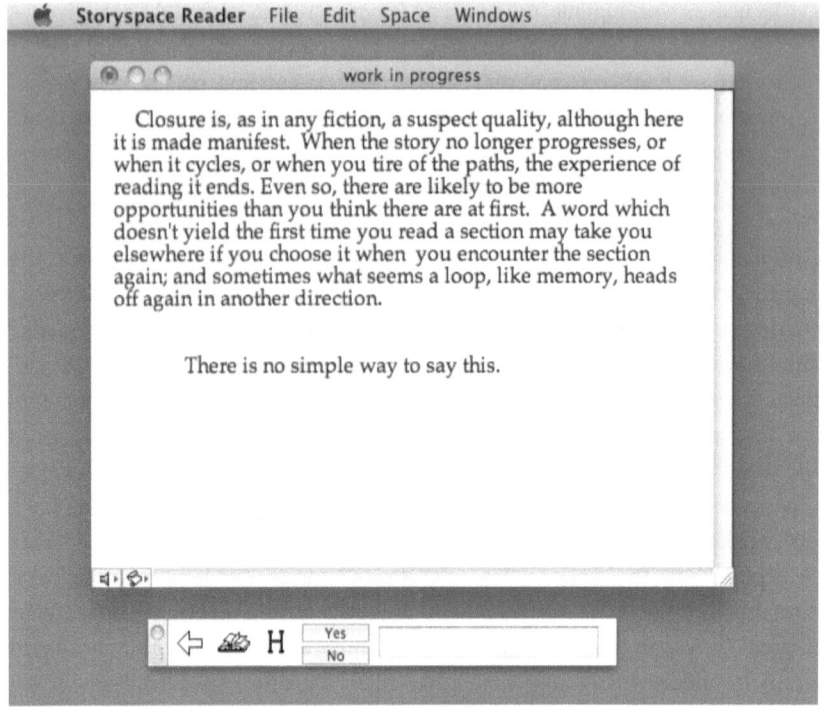

FIGURE 1.1. Michael Joyce, *afternoon*

presented as unique to this storytelling medium, provides a model for describing how the reader comes to grasp textual rules in electronic narratives in general. In coining this term, Aarseth hopes to save games from their "colonization" by narrative study, and so it should be no surprise that he rejects the idea that when maneuvering through interactive fiction we are simply getting a traditional story in a somewhat more complex and challenging way. For him, "there is no story at all, in the traditional sense" (*Cybertext* 112), because we can never be sure that the actions that we take while playing will turn out to be narratively significant. Aarseth instead suggests that the concept of intrigue captures the different structure of activity that players/readers engage in when encountering interactive fiction:

> There is nevertheless a structuring element in these texts, which in some ways does the controlling or at least motivates it. As a new term for this element I propose *intrigue*, to suggest a secret plot in which the user is the innocent, but voluntary target (*victim* is too strong a term), with an outcome that is not yet decided—or rather with several possible outcomes that depend on various factors, such as the cleverness and experience of the player. (112)

Aarseth explains that in an ergodic text like interactive fiction, "intrigue is directed against the user, who must figure out for herself what is going on" (113). The target of the intrigue he calls the *intriguee* to parallel the *narratee*, and the entity responsible for creating the whole structure he names the *intrigant*, as a parallel to the *narrator*. I depart from Aarseth's handling of the concept by seeing the structure of intrigue as independent, parallel and complementary to narration. Aarseth's goal is to offer an alternative to traditional narrative terms; we are caught in an intrigue to the extent that we are not experiencing a story, he claims. My suggestion, instead, is to see intrigue as a component of all electronic texts and to recognize that those texts may, nonetheless, also have narrative elements like narrators and narratees. Indeed, I think that intrigue becomes even more interesting when combined with traditional narrative elements—as we have seen in the complex layering of voices and readerly roles in *afternoon*'s "work in progress" lexia.

In his recent book, *Refiguring Minds in Narrative Media,* David Ciccoricco has analyzed this feature of digital narrative as well. He agrees about the central features of this dynamic: "Thus, to account for the additional recursive exchange between reader and computer in all digital fiction and the way in which the machine regulates and contours our reading experience, we can attribute the operational output of digital narratives to a cybernetic narrator or to a process of cybernetic narration" (77). He argues that the intrigant is specific to the adventure game, and that "it does not readily apply across other forms and genres of digital fiction" because it "necessitates an adversarial engagement" (78). Although he is certainly correct that Aarseth's formulation emphasizes the adversarial relationship with the player, Ciccoricco and I share an interest in finding a way to discuss the theoretical entity that appears to have designed the mechanical elements of the work. And, in fact, the intrigant *is* the entity that puts the reader in a position where he or she has to act, and so retaining intrigue's implication that the user is being challenged by the text seems appropriate to me. He argues that we should assign the mechanical elements of the text like hypertext links to the cybernetic narrator, while I am suggesting that we retain Aarseth's somewhat quirky concept of the intrigant. As this book goes on, we will see that this entity applies to other aspects of the text's construction, and not just to narration.

Ciccoricco's theory of cybernetic narration does, however, raise a crucial issue for my suggestion that we adopt the intrigue/intrigant/intriguee structure as an additional layer within the electronic text. His approach calls for a unity of intrigue and narration under the control of a single cybernetic narrator: "Cybernetic narration thus provides an economic way to coherently integrate the thematic and programmatic design of digital fiction" (80). Narrative theorists are, of course, rightly wary about calls to people with text with an ever-expanding population of narrative entities responsible for different elements of the text. This, after all, is the basis for Walsh's critique of distinguishing an extradiegetic homodiegetic narrator from other characters. By subordinating the programmatic and narrative design of the work to a single entity (the cybernetic narrator), Ciccoricco adopts a theoretically more parsimonious stance on the structure of the digital text. I would argue, however, that there are two reasons to indulge the proliferation of theoretical entities in the digital text.

First, more than almost any other medium, digital narrative is very often a combination of two different creative impulses: one storytelling, and the other what Ciccoricco calls textual "architectonics." This is especially the case when a particular text adopts user interface components that are deployed in other works. It is easy to see this in the case of the Storyspace system that I have cited just above in *afternoon,* but it is perhaps even more the case in commercial video game development, where a particular studio might adopt off-the-shelf technologies for part of their design. The Unity game engine is a particularly well-known example of this kind of tool that provides a way to render three-dimensional spaces on-screen, freeing programmers from the low-level task of telling the computer how to display and update our view of these spaces. Such tools are common: from the SCUMM utility (script creation utility form Maniac Mansion) used by LucasArts in its influential early graphic adventure games, through Twine, an accessible tool for creating web-based hyperlinked texts. Of course, there are many other forms of narrative that involve creative partnerships. I have already noted what Seymour Chatman describes as "Authorship by Committee" is the big-studio film (*Coming to Terms* 90). Although we tend to use the director as a short-hand for the creative impulse behind the film, we recognize that what we actually see on-screen is a combination of the work of the actors, the cinematographer, the sound designer, producers, and editors—even leaving aside the higher-level commercial constraints that the studio might put on a production. But precisely because these individuals and forces are so dispersed and variable, reverting to a single "implied author" (the director) is a worthwhile theoretical assumption. In the digital text, conversely, there is often a clearer bifurcation between the design of the intrigue and the authoring of the story. Indeed, often games depend on separate genres and formulas for storyworld and gameplay: a Star Wars 3D shooter, a detective text adventure game, or a superhero 2D platformer. We can bring some parallel categories to bear on film, such as our knowledge of the film stock or camera technology, but it is much less common to see these as the result of a separate design decision.

Second, I believe that adopting the terms *intriguee* and *intrigant* provides us with language to talk about particular features of these digital narratives. I hope that the examples that follow will demonstrate this utility, but the example of *afternoon* already suggests the direction of my discussion. It is possible to see the same creative entity as responsible both for the narration that refers to "A word which doesn't yield" and the user interface buttons below, but our experience of interacting with this text involves a subtle shift in attitude that is comparable but not reducible to the shift between character and authorial audience. Joyce, as well, encourages us to see the literary content of the work as somewhat disengaged from the mechanics of the user interface by evoking this metaphorical language to describe narration. It is a shift from pretending to read a story (bringing to bear all the knowledge that we have as the authorial audience) to discovering the mechanics of our interaction with the interface of the digital work, and is distinctive of digital narrative. As my discussion below moves away from the explicitly literary example of *afternoon*, I think that the descriptive value of the terms *intriguee* and *intrigant* will become clearer. I will end this chapter, however, with a discussion of intrigue as a component of the work even if we decide to jettison these two supporting theoretical entities.

THREE EXAMPLES

In this section, I explore a variety of case studies that illustrate the analytic advantages of distinguishing between narration and intrigue in electronic narratives.

Let us begin with interactive fictions, since Aarseth developed his theory of intrigue on the basis of this subcorpus of electronic narratives. Initially, the reader's positioning in interactive fiction seems to be identical to that of second-person narration in print, since in both cases, the reader is described as "you." In particular, the player character in these stories seems very much an instance of what James Phelan has described as a "characterized audience": "a characterized audience is created whenever a narrator, using direct address, ascribes attributes to his or her audience. From the perspective of the narrative audience, the characterized audience may be either real or hypothetical—that is, it may be an actual character such as Shreve McCanlin in *Absalom, Absalom!* or any number of figures in epistolary novels, or it may be a construction of the narrator such as the various Sirs and Madams invented by Tristram Shandy" (136). In some ways, *characterized audience* is merely another way of describing the narratee (139), but Phelan's articulation emphasizes the potential tension between characterized and narrative audiences. In the case of *If on a Winter's Night a Traveller*, for example, Phelan notes that Calvino's strategy is to "vary the thickness of the screen between the narrator and the narrative audience erected by the use of the characterized audience" (142). This tension is particularly rich in interactive fiction, since these games will often attribute far greater specificity to the player's actions than inputted commands indicate. To take a trivial example, one of the first tasks in the early adventure game *Zork* is to open a window to enter a house. In response to the command "open window" the player is told: "With great effort, you open the window far enough to allow entry." In describing the "great effort" used here, the game characterizes the audience independently of the player's choices.

But this description of the structure of *narration* tells us little about the actions that we must take as the agent responsible for moving the player through the game—that is, the structure of *intrigue* and our role as *intriguee*. In fact, our language for describing what we are *doing* as the player is imprecise. Nick Montfort has critiqued the idea that we are "playing" the character in a theatrical sense in interactive fiction. Montfort notes that

> there is no real role to play, only an existing history that waits to be discovered. The player character can be steered through the station to recover his memory. But the interactor does little more than steer and sense. The author, not the player, is the one who decides when the player will cry, the one who defines all the details of the player character's earlier and more expressive actions and reactions. (141)

In other words, what players must *do* is independent of their identity as the characterized audience. One of the things that makes some early interactive fiction notoriously difficult is that the reader is given a character identity but forced to behave in a way that makes little sense for that character. Take, for example, the influential early game *The Hitchhiker's Guide to the Galaxy*. Although certainly not as aesthetically sophisticated as more recent interactive fiction, this early game reflects particularly clearly the contrast between the roles of characterized audience and intriguee in this genre of electronic writing. At the beginning of this story the player is defined as Arthur Dent asleep in his bedroom, but the player has none of the knowledge about his house or possessions that the character himself could be assumed to have: "You wake up. The room is spinning very gently round your head. Or at least it would be if you could see it which you can't. It is pitch black." Even after standing up, turning on the light, and finding Dent in his own bedroom, the player knows little about the house and possible courses of action. More importantly, as the story progresses successful actions depend less on proper responses to exigencies in the storyworld than on knowledge of the book on which the game is based. Shortly after leaving the bedroom, for example, the player must stop the approach of a bulldozer intended to knock down Dent's house by lying down in its path and waiting for his friend Ford Prefect to appear—a course of action that mimics Adams' original novel, but that would make little sense otherwise. Our responsibilities as intriguee have little to do with pretending to be Dent, the characterized audience; as Monfort says, "the interactor is simply not working very hard to act in a manner particular to a character, as is done when playing a dramatic role" (139). I think that we can push Montfort's observation further and note that the structure of intrigue will be particular in each individual text. In some works of interactive fiction, exploration is central and we are quite literally "steering" the player character through a mysterious location.[2] But in *Hitchhiker's Guide* our role as intriguee is quite different: we are challenged to draw on our knowledge of the original book in order to solve these puzzles. In this sense, the intriguee is not Dent himself, but a fan of Adams' novel, drawing on knowledge of how the story must go in order to progress. Here the gap between characterized audience and intriguee is clear.

Let us return to *afternoon* to see how the distinction between intrigue and narration helps us to understand the dynamics of reader positioning when we no longer have a well-defined characterized audience with which to identify. Critics have noted that the identity of the narrator of various lexia in this story is quite complex. Alice Bell, in particular, has unpacked how Joyce seems to create a third-person narrator only to reveal later that such narration is actually the work of the story's primary, first-person narrator, Peter (43). Other passages (like the "yes6" lexia), however, are narrated from the point of view of Peter's antagonist Wert and refer to Peter in the third person. And even in those passages in which Peter remains the narrator, the narratee changes, shifting between a general narratee and the more specific character that Bell calls Peter's "confidante" (43). Likewise, we have already seen that Joyce muddies the distinction between these narrators and a level of discourse in the story that reflects Joyce's own voice as the story's author. In the "twenty questions" lexia Joyce appears to ask metafictional questions to the reader about the story—"Who is sleeping with whom, and why?"—although the lexia could also represent Peter's self-questioning. Another lexia, "Blowup," refers to the characters in the third person in a voice that seems to be that of the author: "The pure ennui of the industrial landscape not unlike the absentedness of these characters' lives, also broken by occasional passion." Is this Peter reflecting on his own account, or Joyce talking about the story he has written? *Afternoon* seems designed to make such questions impossible to answer.

2. I will return to this idea of steering what Aarseth calls a "puppet" character through the text adventure game in chapter 4.

In contrast to the story's ambiguous narrators, the intrigant is a much more straightforward figure who challenges readers to navigate the world of the narrative with little guidance, and tells them that repetition will be necessary. Our exploration of this work is largely blind, and is the result of an intrigant who clearly wants to frustrate the reader's traditional sense of closure. As we saw with interactive fiction, critics sometimes want to translate the demands that intrigue makes on the reader into those of narration, and to blur the role of intriguee and narratee. In discussing the hidden "white afternoon" lexia, Ryan attempts to provide a motivation for the tasks that the intrigant has given us: "This sequence suggests that the dialogue with the therapist unlocked guilt feelings in the narrator or led to a more lucid self-awareness" (*Avatars* 138). Joyce himself made a similar observation about the story in a conversation with Douglas: "In order to physically get to 'white afternoon,' you have to go through therapy with Lolly, the way Peter does" (100). This explanation is suggestive, but ultimately misleading. While the story's intrigue may have a metaphorical similarity to the events of the story—our working through of these associations is in some ways *like* being in therapy—trying to find out what happened in the story eventually becomes a matter of following links until we feel we understand their design principle. Douglas makes this clear in her explanation of why she felt she had "completed" *afternoon*: "*my interpretation of the significance of 'white afternoon' is tied to my perception of 'I call' as a central junction in the structure of the text and of 'white afternoon' as a peripheral, deeply embedded and relatively inaccessible place*" (105). Douglas describes her reading not as a narratee being addressed by Peter, but as an intriguee challenged to uncover the structural rules for the text. Although hidden, this design has none of the ambiguity we see in the story's narration.

Afternoon's construction of intrigue and narration is especially striking when we compare it to another hypertext work, Shelly Jackson's *Patchwork Girl*. Since both works were created using Eastgate's Storyspace program, we would expect the design of intrigue to be largely the same, but in fact the nature of the intrigue is quite different. Granted, the structure of the narration in *Patchwork Girl* has superficial similarities to *afternoon*. Like *afternoon*, Jackson's story depends on several narrators (the monster, its creator, Jackson herself), but intersperses personal stories with broader, more philosophical reasoning; thus the lexia titled "resurrection" begins: "The human, more than human resurrected body is a body restored to wholeness and perfection, even to a perfection it never achieved in its original state." But while *afternoon*'s narration mixes heterogeneous elements to create confusion, *Patchwork Girl*'s variations of style tend to reflect the movement between broad and specific commentary on the text's core concerns. Hayles notes that Jackson's use of links is "argumentative" (154) and that she frequently uses the transition between lexias to provide commentary on other texts—as when she reprints Mary Shelley's 1831 preface to the novel and provides the monster's comments (156). In designing the text's intrigue, Jackson made her story easy to navigate. She reveals the structure of the text by providing a Storyspace "map," and creates a central launching point for the story based on a series of metaphorical characterizations of the text: a graveyard, a journal, a quilt, a story, "& broken accents." The movement between lexias is more coherent and easier to predict; even jumps between narrators are less confusing than in *afternoon* because the reader's task is considering these issues rather than understanding the design principle for the work and revealing relatively inaccessible lexias. Yet as with *afternoon* there is a homology between the design of the intrigue and the design of the narration: just as the story provides a central starting point based around core metaphors to which the reader can always return, so too the narration appears to move between poetic comparisons and more specific, almost essayistic, reflections on what is going on.

I would like to turn to one more example that shows how narration and intrigue can form distinct but complementary textual systems in electronic narratives. The work that I have in mind is a short electronic text called *Outrances*, which was published at the online *Born Magazine*. This journal explicitly describes its works as "collaborative" and its editorial challenge as "matchmaking" a relationship between writer and designer; it frequently produces interactive electronic "interpretations" of poems previously published in print. When *Outrances* launches, we are greeted with a screen showing the interface designers Scott Ichikawa and James Dvorak holding a photograph of the textual author, Thomas H. Crofts III. Ichikawa and Dvorak are dressed casually and are caught yelling rambunctiously, while the picture of Crofts shows him as the stereotypical dour author, dressed in a tie and smoking a pipe (see figure 1.2). The opening of the work reminds readers forcefully and ironically that the text has two separate sources: author and designer.

Crofts's original, 20-line poem is divided into two halves; the first narrates being awakened from private immersion in music on a cassette tape, and the second shifts to the "crowds some sworling host" affected by music. The context of these events is obscure and no reference is made to the audience directly. Instead, we are encouraged by an epigraph describing a band performance to reflect on the poem's theme of losing oneself in music. As the authorial audience we might notice the work's striking abruptness and refusal to provide context for these reflections as itself an example of the poem's account of aesthetic disorientation. Turning to the user's responsibilities as intriguee, we find a structure of intrigue that has great metaphorical but little literal connection to the story we are told about being lost in music. *Outrances* places the text of this poem on physical objects amid the detritus of urban life. The text is placed onto the sort of handmade, photocopied posters that would be used to advertise the performance of a local band. These posters are glued onto every sort of surface—from designated community bulletin boards to dumpsters and the sides of buildings (see figure 1.3).

The work moves forward through the city, zooming in on one poster after another, pausing long enough for the user to read the text, and then zooming out to move on to another location in the city. In fact, the reader often cannot immediately tell where the text of the poem will be in a particular scene, since such handmade posters litter the landscape; it is only when the work zooms in on the particular words of the poem, cropping out other bits of text, that those words are revealed to the reader. As intriguee, the reader is positioned as an explorer of urban life, gradually discovering poetry amid the seeming chaos of the landscape. The reader is not asked to choose a path here, but merely to recognize the text when it appears. In *Outrances,* narration and intrigue are connected thematically: both are concerned with finding order in chaos, with losing oneself in art, and with the process of connecting to and differentiating oneself from crowds. Here narration and intrigue are independent but thematically complementary textual systems.

FIGURE 1.2. Scott Ichikawa, Thomas H. Crofts, and James Dvorak, *Outrances* (photograph)

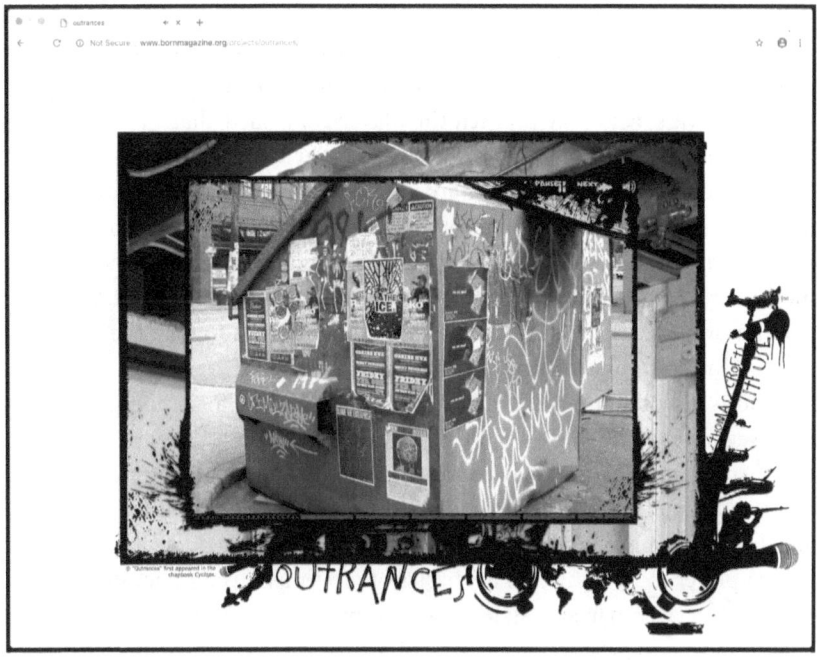

FIGURE 1.3. Scott Ichikawa, Thomas H. Crofts, and James Dvorak, *Outrances* (posters)

CHARACTERS, NARRATORS, AND INTRIGUE IN VIDEO GAMES

Thus far in this chapter, I have focused on digital works that are clear examples of electronic literature, works that are fundamentally based on text and reading. This is a natural place to focus, since in these works there is a clear role for the narrator, which makes the contrast with the intrigant clearer. I would argue, however, that intrigue is a useful term even in nontextual cases where we do not have a clear narrator's voice with which to contrast it.

In *Transmedial Narratology and Contemporary Media Culture*, Jan-Noël Thon provides a useful analysis of ways that video games handle narration that suggests a broader application of the concept of intrigue. In particular, he adopts a looser understanding of narrational activity as applying to the various ways that information is conveyed to the player, even if that comes from on-screen characters rather than a narrator. He notes that narration has to "fulfill both narrative and ludic functions" (207). These ludic functions can include game mechanics (literally, how to move the character or use equipment), but also more broadly about player goals that allow the story to move forward. Narration can be handled directly by cut-scenes that often involve either a hetero- or homodiegetic narrator (208–9). More interesting is the way that non-player characters (NPCs) can function like narrators, "from primarily narrative, when other characters fill the player-controlled character in on recent (or not so recent) events, to primarily ludic, when other characters act as 'quest-givers' who may also tell the player-controlled character what happened subsequently, but do so primarily in order to ask him or her for help" (209). Of course, these characters are not literally narrators or intrigants; they do, however, help to further the work of narration and intrigue. Thon's discussion emphasizes a point that I have made in this chapter as well: that the ludic mechanics of the game complicate our understanding of narration. When we read a novel, we hardly need the narrator to remind us to turn the page, nor does a film need to tell us to keep watching the screen.

Thon's discussion of video game narration is helpful for reminding us that even seemingly straightforward narrational voices can address the mechanics of the game. Most games strive to keep the semblance of a distinction between character narration and directions from what I am calling the intrigant. In the opening minutes of first-person adventure games, it is common for the player to be trained in the basics of movement using a combination of character or even narrator statements and mechanical directions about what keys to push—sometimes presented as a visual overlay to distinguish between character and intrigant voice. A good example is the character creation screen for the influential fantasy game *Morrowind*. A few minutes into the game, the player meets a guard who remarks, "You finally arrived, but our records don't show from where" (see figure 1.4). This immediately brings up a character creation screen in which the player is asked to choose a race, a gender, and to make some tweaks to their character's appearance (see figure 1.5). This example clearly involves the playful movement between character voice (the guard) and a shift towards what appears to be the intrigant addressing the player directly as the intriguee in the character customization panel, which essentially translates that in-game question into a mechanical feature of the game's operation. As Thon makes clear, video games tend to rely on player dialog and narration for this kind of information. But we have seen the same shift between narrator voice and interface design in hypertext narrative as well. In fact, the gap between the guard's dialog and the character customization panel is exactly the same as that between Joyce's general narrator's description of *afternoon* and the specific navigational options in the larger user interface that go unmentioned by the narrator.

In *Gaming*, Alexander Galloway argues that video games represent the point of contact between player and machine actions. He gives several examples: "Locating a power-up in *Super Mario Bros.* is an operator act, but the power-up actually boosting the player character's health is a machine act" (5). It is clear that what I have described as the voice of the intrigant can be seen

FIGURE 1.4. Narration from a guard character in *Morrowind*.

FIGURE 1.5. Character customization prompt in *Morrowind*.

as the act of the machine speaking directly to the player about how to perform some action using the game's user interface. Indeed, as in the interface of *afternoon*, the intrigant communicates directly to the player, often over the head of other narrators and characters. And as the self-conscious cleverness of the shift from the voice of the character and the voice of the interface in *Morrowind* suggests, the interaction between these two voices has a significant impact on our experience of these works.

DO WE NEED THE INTRIGANT AND INTRIGUEE?

In my discussion of these examples, I hope to have demonstrated the complexity of reader positioning in digital narrative. This complexity is not unique to the electronic medium; Choose Your Own Adventure and children's pop-up books likewise create an intriguee role for their readers. But the electronic medium makes these possibilities more central to the experience of these texts. We gain considerably by seeing intrigue as a structure that exists amid the familiar dynamics of author, narrator, and reader; this approach provides a way to talk about the overlapping and potentially contradictory roles that readers take on when engaging with these texts. At times readers are part of the narrative audience, at times they shift to look at the story from the point of view of the authorial audience, and throughout they are aware of the task of being the intriguee charged with navigating the work. But my larger point is that factoring in the concepts of intrigue, intrigant, and intriguee allows the voices and roles at play in a work like *afternoon* to be explored in a more fine-grained, nuanced way. Obviously, my argument for the existence of a system of intrigue alongside the structure of narration leaves many elements of this relationship still somewhat unexplored. In electronic narratives, does it make sense to postulate an implied designer alongside an implied author, or to distinguish between an intradiegetic and heterodiegetic intrigant? How does the difference between the intradiegetic narratee that we see in interactive fiction and the (largely) extradiegetic narratee that we see in *Patchwork Girl* affect how we recognize our responsibilities as intriguee? I do believe, however, that common narrative distinctions might be extended to the structure of intrigue. Consider the instructions for the tongue-in-cheek game *Plants vs. Zombies*, in which players are charged with defending their home by deploying plants that shoot, immobilize, or eat waves of onrushing zombies. If the player selects the *help* button, the game provides the following instructions: "When the Zombies show up, just sit there and don't do anything. You win the game when the Zombies get to your houze [sic]." In smaller print, the reason for this poor advice is explained: "this help section brought to you by the Zombies." Here we seem to have a dramatized, homodiegetic, intrigant who is moreover unreliable. Although there are obviously many elements of the relationship between intrigue and narration to be explored, there is every reason to think that these core narrative structures and roles will resonate with each other.

By applying the concept of intrigue from the text adventure to digital narrative generally, this chapter also suggests that it may have applications to other media. Any text that plays with its form as a physical object is likely to manifest an intrigant address at some stage. Some children's books are quite explicit in addressing readers as intriguees—"Turn the page to find out!" The Choose Your Own Adventure books are an obvious case as well, and have long served as physical analogs to later digital works. In fact, the well-known example of the Sesame Street children's book *The Monster at the End of This Book* shows clearly that intrigue can apply directly and in sophisticated ways to print texts. In this story, Grover pleads with the reader not to turn any pages after he reads the title and is frightened: "Listen, I have an idea. If you do not turn any pages, we will never get to the end of this book. And that is good, because there is a Monster at the end of it" (n.pag.). Obviously, the reader continues to turn pages, and Grover erects fictional barriers (like a brick wall) designed to stop progress. Although this book is often cited when discussing casual or popular metafiction, Grover's voice is surprisingly complex. Clearly, he shares the intriguee role with the actual reader, and is thus subject to the design and conditions of the book constructed by someone else (the intrigant) who has "put" the monster at the end of the book. Indeed, Grover's "plan" just summarized above is an example of the way that the intriguee must learn the rules of the work in order to decide how to use them strategically. But it is clear, as well, that Grover is also "in" the book, and that his actions are limited by the fact that he is not able to alter the book as an artifact itself; instead, all that he can do is create fictional obstructions and plead with the reader. He is clearly a dramatized intriguee, in some ways parallel to the narratee. But the narratee's counterpart is the narrator, and both are entities contained entirely in the work, whereas the idea of dramatizing and representing an intriguee is inherently a matter of crossing ontological boundaries.[3]

As these examples make clear, any work that relies on instructions to the reader of the physical book introduces another voice that performs similarly

---

3. In fact, the surprise ending of the book is that it is Grover himself who is the "monster" at the end. One way to read this is to say that Grover imagines himself as a reader of the book, but eventually discovers that he is part of the book world as his actions have no effect on the book as a physical artifact. In other words, he starts the book believing that he is an intriguee but eventually discovers that he is simply a character.

to the intrigant. Often such instructions are associated with a fictional editor, as in the case of Milorad Pavić's *Dictionary of the Khazars*, which contains a section called "How to Use the Dictionary" as part of a fictional "preliminary notes." In cases where such textual instructions are not associated with a particular person in the story, the concept of an intrigue is particularly useful. A clear example is Julio Cortázar's *Hopscotch*, which opens with a "Table of Instructions" explaining the two ways that the book can be read. Although the voice here is far from neutral and is definitely characterized—referring to the "three garish little stars which stand for the words *The End*" on the last page of chapter 56—the tendency is to associate it with Cortázar directly. The possibility of a tension between the narrator of the text and the instructions given in these kinds of paratextual statements has not attracted the scholarly attention that it deserves, outside of cases where they are associated with a characterized editor such as in *Pale Fire* or *House of Leaves*. Digital narratives make clear that it is possible to have a tension between the voice of the intrigant and the voice of the narrator even in cases where there is no character editor or person otherwise described as assembling the book.

Earlier in this chapter I noted a justifiable suspicion among narrative theorists about calls to add additional theoretical entities responsible for aspects of a narrative. I hope that I have demonstrated the nature of intrigue as a feature of these digital texts that requires the reader to act in certain ways. It is clear that the same narration coupled with a different form of intrigue would produce a very different kind of experience. It is, of course, possible to embrace intrigue as a theoretical concept without positing separate entities responsible for creating and acting on it. That is, in the interest of keeping our theoretical concepts as spare as possible, we could argue that digital texts have an implied author who creates both the narration and the intrigue, and that both are directed towards an implied reader/player who is the object of both narration and intrigue. I have already argued earlier that the conditions for the production of digital texts, particularly the common practice of using the same tools and engines for rendering graphics and other features of the interface, makes digital narratives more likely to be the product of the collaboration of two distinct creative forces. It is a fair question, nonetheless, if ignoring these conditions of production in favor of unified implied author would lose any significant explanatory power.

Having looked at these examples above, I hope to have demonstrated the value of retaining the intriguee as a way to describe the shift that the reader or player must make between experiencing the text as a story and processing it as an artifact that must be operated effectively. The simple example of *Morrowind* shows this at work, as the player shifts from a narrational situation about the character's origins, to an interface that contains features specific to the game's mechanics. It is only after this dialog pops up that the player understands the range and limits of character customization—something that has nothing to do with the storytelling situation. Games particularly depend on this kind of dual consciousness, since effective gameplay can often require being able to translate the story into the rules of play. In the case of *The Hitchhiker's Guide to the Galaxy* discussed above, the player has to do a particular kind of mental shift that is quite different from what we see in changing from the narrative to the authorial audience: translating the story being told into a puzzle to be solved by using knowledge of the original book. Indeed, that disengagement from the story being told is one of the challenges and pleasures of these digital narratives, where a player may have to ignore the story being told (you have fallen in among a horde of enemies) for the sake of gameplay mechanics (what is going to trigger the start of the fight?). The case of *afternoon* is particularly significant here, since Joyce seems to want to separate the storytelling situation from the mechanical interface that the reader uses, and to present an authorial identity that is more traditionally literary. Of course it is possible to expand the notion of an authorial audience to include all the information about the design of the program and gameplay, and there are times when the gap between authorial and narrative audience is quite large. But the double-consciousness required by digital narratives, which much more consistently separate narrative from the mechanics of the interface and gameplay, is better captured by positing an intrigant and intriguee alongside the narrator and narratee.

We have also seen that the intrigant and the intriguee are valuable in giving us a way to describe when these aspects of the digital narrative are characterized. The examples of *The Monster at the End of This Book* and *Plants vs. Zombies* give us a characterized intriguee and intrigant, respectively. We could perhaps talk about Grover as a particular kind of narratee that is both reading the text as each page turns, but referring to him as an intriguee more accurately captures his attempt to learn and exploit the rules of the story's progression—its intrigue. And the titular Zombies in their game are unreliable, characterized intrigants, giving the player bad advice about how to play the game. Of course, unreliable intrigants are not common, so we might conclude that building a model for digital narrative around these edge cases is unwise. But Thon shows that it is common for players to take on the role of helping players to figure out the design of the intrigue, and the terms intrigant and intriguee give us a way to talk about these common shifts in narrative and gameplay roles.

CHAPTER 2

Space across Narrative Media

IF NARRATION represents one of the core and inescapable elements of narrative theory, setting is a rather neglected aspect of storytelling. Although Joseph Frank's 1945 essay "Spatial Form in Modern Literature" argued that the construction of space could be a fundamental element of the aesthetic design of narrative, it was not until the 1980s when there was a sustained interest in developing a typology of narrative space. This new attention to space was prompted in part by Bakhtin's essay on the chronotope (which received its modern translation into English in 1981), and in part by the widespread interest in structuralism and the general use of space as an organizing principle for meaning. More recently, cognitive approaches to narrative have renewed interest in space precisely because it seems so important for how we make sense of things in the world and in fiction. In *Story Logic,* for example, David Herman analyzes "how narratives enable (or in some cases inhibit) 'cognitive mapping,' the process by which things and events are mentally modeled as being located somewhere in the world" (265). Among the many commonly discussed concepts in narrative theory, space is unusual in generating consistent interest while at the same time never quite coalescing into a well-defined series of terms and debates.

It is a natural place to turn in this book, however, because digital media prioritizes space so strongly. Our language for computing is dominated by the idea of window and screen.[1] It is no surprise that Jay David Bolter's early (1991) book on writing and hypertext was called *Writing Space*, since the screen as the site of action is central to so much of our understanding of electronic textuality. Although media like print and film are spatial as well—the page of the novel is a space, after all—digital media require a constant awareness of the spatiality of the screen. Screen space is often made up of regions with which we interact differently (menus, palates), and we often have to pay close attention to changes in the position of items (a change of state, notification, or movement of an avatar), while in the vast majority of printed texts the spatial positioning of individual words is irrelevant. Simply put, for nearly all digital media, we encounter the work through a screen that itself must be designed by someone—the intrigant, we can say, to use the term developed in chapter 1. As a result, it provides a powerful way to examine our theories of narrative space.

PRIMARY AND ORIENTING SPACES IN DIGITAL NARRATIVE

I would like to focus on a core feature of space in digital narrative, which is most obvious in commercial video games: the distinction between game spaces where players can act, or primary spaces, and those spaces that are part of the gameworld in a more abstract way, or orienting spaces. In every modern three-dimensional video game, players understand that there are limits to the spaces the player avatar can inhabit and affect. Most games strive to provide a realistic justification for these limits by bounding player movement through natural features of geography (a cliff that cannot be scaled, a dramatic walkway edge that forces the player down a certain path); relying on "invisible walls" that arbitrarily stop player movement is a common sign of poor game design.

Many early arcade games are nothing but primary space—we might think about the classic *Pac-Man*, in which there appears to be no larger world in which the gameplay maze is set. Most modern games orient these playable spaces within a larger non-playable space. The most common manifestation of such non-playable spaces is a secondary map that locates primary spaces within a larger world, and often provides a means by which the player can jump from one primary space to another, such as in *Baldur's Gate* (see figure 2.1). Frequently this world space is associated with a set of missions, so that by moving to individual playable locations the player is implicitly selecting

---

[1]. For a discussion of the metaphor of the computer window in relation to other ways of thinking about representational space, such as the painting as a window and the cinematic screen, see Anne Friedberg's *The Virtual Window: From Alberti to Microsoft*.

FIGURE 2.1. *Baldur's Gate*

tasks to be completed. In *Mass Effect 2*, for example, a map nominally on the bridge of the space ship Normandy is used by the player to travel to different locations and start or continue missions (see figure 2.2). In each of these cases, players are interacting with a fundamentally different notion of space than they encounter within the main game.

In more abstract, puzzle-like games the role of this orienting space can sometimes be quite whimsical, and obey the logic of a larger world space only in the most general way. For example, the early iOS game *Zen Bound* involves spinning a three-dimensional wooden model in order to wrap it in string. To move between different models, which have different challenges, users are presented with a Japanese-style garden tree holding different objects (see figure 2.3). To select a particular puzzle in this game, users merely tap on one of the objects on the tree. As this example makes clear, sometimes an

FIGURE 2.2. Mass Effect 2

FIGURE 2.3. *Zen Bound 2*

orienting space functions as little more than a game menu—although one that is stylistically consistent with the material emphasis in the main gameplay space. Although I have focused thus far on games, these kinds of orienting spaces are common in literary digital narrative as well. Literary hypertexts frequently make use of an orienting object that provides a secondary spatial reference for the reading experience. Shelley Jackson's *Patchwork Girl* is perhaps the most obvious example of a work that depends on a second kind of space—the parts of the body in one instance, or the phrenology of the skull in another—to orient individual reading passages within an artistic whole.

These kinds of orienting spaces can, then, take on the form of a represented object that provides the frame for gameplay. Probably the best early example of this is the visual designs that surrounded the gameplay space of the early-90s Tetris, which did nothing to create a coherent world space but instead provided a kind of baroque decoration for the unused screen space (see figure 2.4).

This decorative framing is common in explicitly literary digital works as well. Roderick Coover's *Voyage into the Unknown* offers readers a huge map-like space through which they must scroll. This space initially (to the leftmost) relies on map-like elements (trees, rivers) with more expressive coloring, but as readers move rightward, the space is dominated by images of the landscape against a horizon (see figure 2.5).

Readers can access brief prose passages by selecting some of these images. It is clear that this orienting space is not meant to be consistent with the spaces implied by the textual passages in any literal way; instead there is a metaphorical and expressive relationship between these two kinds of space. This more expressive or decorative framing space is common in digital literary works that draw their inspiration from games, such as Jason Nelson's use of repurposed commercial websites as background in *i made this. you play this. we are enemies* (see figure 2.6).

Likewise, such framing is common in works closer to the tradition of concrete poetry, where words move into a space to be read. We might think of *Born Magazine* coauthored examples such as *Don't Be Afraid to Help Sharks* or *A Servant. A Hanging. A Paper House* (see figure 2.7).

FIGURE 2.4. *Tetris*

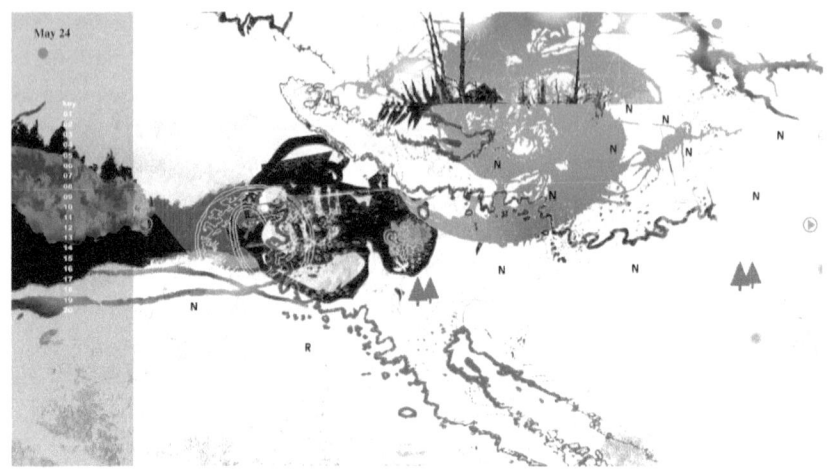

FIGURE 2.5. Roderick Coover, *Voyage into the Unknown*

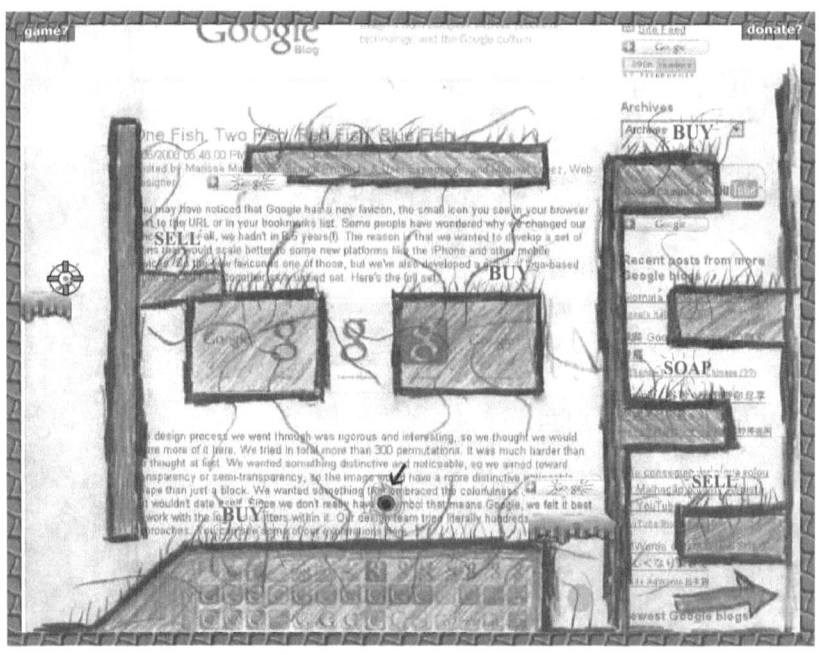

FIGURE 2.6. Jason Nelson, *i made this. you play this. we are enemies.*

FIGURE 2.7. Lucy Anderton and Nicholas Robinson, *A Servant. A Hanging. A Paper House.*

As this example makes clear, the distinction between primary and orienting space can extend far beyond the spaces of video games. The computer desktop metaphor itself is essentially a primary space for action (where folders can be created, files moved, and so on) and a much smaller orienting space (a menu or toolbar) that provides information and context for your actions. In chapter 4 I will discuss the representation of action in player avatars and Britta Neitzel's use of the term "point of action" as an alternative to point of view that can encompass, for example, the mouse pointer. Although my emphasis here is on games and literary texts, it should be clear that the distinction between spaces of context and spaces of action can be extended to nearly any piece of software.

In summary, then, primary spaces are those of action—either the literal space in which a player controls an avatar in a game, or the space of narration in a work like *Voyage into the Unknown*. Orienting spaces provide a context for those primary spaces by allowing the player to choose missions, helping the reader to see a larger world that connects the various primary spaces, or by providing a thematic or artistic framework for understanding the events in the primary space. As such, this kind of space is not common in print and other media.

NARRATOLOGICAL DIMENSIONS OF SPACE IN PRINT NARRATIVE

To understand what is new in the spaces of digital narrative, it is helpful to compare them to more traditional theories of setting. For a sophisticated account of setting and the way it is defined by other spaces in the narrative, we might begin with Ruth Ronen's "Space in Fiction." Ronen offers the central concept of the "frame" for thinking about narrative space. For her, "A frame is a fictional place, the actual or potential surrounding of fictional characters, objects, and places. [. . .] Various expressions in the text construct different types of frames which compose the global structure of the space of a story" (421). As this implies, the "global structure" of space can be intuited by the reader in a number of ways, including both direct and indirect expressions of the space. She reserves the term "setting" for what she calls the "zero point where the *actual* story-events and story-states are localized" (423). From here she classifies frames in terms of their relationship to this primary space. She refers to the immediate frame as the setting, and secondary frames as background space "constructed close to the setting but distinguished from it by some dividing line" (426). She also identifies three other frames: inaccessible, distant, and generalized. Inaccessible frames "are those which [. . .] are not actualized as immediate surroundings because they cannot be, or are not entered by characters whose actions the narrative follows" (426), while distant frames are "beyond the spatial or temporal boundaries of the story-space or the story-time" (427). Although Ronen's definition of generalized spaces is a little more opaque, she explains that they can include "a class of frames" or a "summarized" space (428), as we might invoke when a character is said to be wandering in the desert in general without specifying a particular geographical location. I find Ronen's account of setting particularly relevant to my discussion of digital narrative because she clearly articulates a distinction between a primary space and those others surrounding it, although her focus is more on classification and less on what these other spaces contribute to the reading experience.

Ronen's essay clearly explains how setting is defined by other spaces in narrative, but neglects some of the complexity that arises from both the textual and temporal way that we encounter this space. In "Towards a Theory of Space in Narrative," Gabriel Zoran tackles both of these issues. He remarks that our ways of talking about space in narrative are frequently metaphorical and lack the specificity of narrative's more literal temporality. To combat this theoretical looseness, Zoran posits a three-level structure of narrative space (315). The *topographical* level understands space as a static entity that we gradually come to reconstruct over the course of reading. The *chronotopic* level treats space through events and movements in the story: "Space, in its topographical structure, is all potential—it is neutral, with regard to any specific movement [. . .]. In contrast, the *chronotopos* determines defined directions in space: in the space of a given narrative, one may move from point *a* to point *b*, but *not* vice versa; in another narrative, the movement may be reversible" (318–19). And the *textual* level shows space as it is articulated within the verbal text itself. Although Zoran describes the topographical level as the "highest" in the sense that it is the most abstracted from the details of the text and plot, he insists that readers constantly move between these levels while reading (315).

I would like to focus on the way that Zoran describes spaces forming the "complex of space" and ultimately the "total space" of the work, since those points are especially relevant to the dual structure of digital narrative. He describes a "horizontal" scheme for the way that the three vertical levels of space just described are connected into larger structures. Zoran's scheme is remarkably complex, so it can be somewhat difficult to keep his terms straight. Each level of the text's space has different basic units that, in turn, are organized into the *complex* of space and the *total space* for each level: "Within the three levels of spatial structure discussed above, a scene on the topographical level is a *place*, on the chronotopical level a *zone of action*, and on the textual level a *field of vision*" (323). Place in this sense describes what we would think of as traditional settings, and could be associated with particular physical locations: "houses, cities, streets, fields" and so on (323). A zone of action, in contrast, is defined not by a physical space but by a relationship between events; Zoran's example is that of a telephone conversation, which can take place in a "discontinuous space" (323). Essentially, Zoran describes how each of these units are structured within each of the text's three levels of space.

Especially important and nuanced is Zoran's account of the field of vision, and it is the way these fields of visions form a larger space that is the most complex and, I think, problematic element of this theory. For Zoran, the field of vision cannot be reduced simply to a single-person point of view in the way that we might when discussing a scene through focalization:

> The field of vision of the text is thus different from the ordinary optical field of vision. The text may refer to an entire city as a field of vision, to a split event (such as a telephone conversation), to a complete battlefield, to a complete house (disregarding the walls which divide its rooms), etc. Naturally, there is also the possibility of following optical rules of perception in a field of vision, but this is only one convention among others and is no more "natural" for the field of vision than the convention of linear perspective is for a drawing. (324)

Zoran sees the narrative as a sequence of fields of vision: "The field of vision is thus to a certain extent the point of intersection between the 'here' of space and the 'now' of the text. It is a unit of reconstructed space which has a correlative in the verbal text: it may be located and identified both within the text and within the world" (327). He asserts that the shift from one field of vision happens "most obviously, [when] there [is] a break, such as a chapter or section ending" (328), and that we can never have two fields of vision operating at any one time in the narrative (328–9). As a result, Zoran sees narrative as essentially a series of fields of vision encountered over the course of reading, which the reader must construct through memory into a larger space.

Zoran's account of the field of vision is powerful precisely because it eschews simple topographical boundaries, and instead tries to develop a model of space that is sensitive to time and aware that narrative space may not simply map onto concrete, unique locations. At the topographical level, total space is relatively specific; he explains that text will build up space through localization in different ways: "Place of events may be located precisely by street and house number, or in a very general way—by the name of the city or county, or even less than this. Each of these cases implies a different way of coordination within total space" (330). The field of vision, however, defines total space as encompassing everything both presented and implied in the text:

> This information, apart from being indirect, is sparse in relation to the information about the complex of space. One of the prominent qualities of total space is the immense domain of missing information. All that can be said about it, both on the basis of textual hints and on the basis of a general knowledge of the external field of reference—all that does not abolish its indeterminacy. (331–2)

The field of vision here includes not only what is actually mentioned or invoked in the text, but also all those elements about real-world space that could be brought to bear to make sense of the narrative. The issue of how much we can fill in the background of a narrative with real-world knowledge has, of course, been a long-running debate within narrative theory. We might recall Marie-Laure Ryan's "principle of minimal departure": we construe the central world of a textual universe "as conforming as far as possible to our representation of" the actual world (*Possible Worlds* 51). Even this strong argument for carrying over our knowledge of the real world into the fictional recognizes limitations. For example, Ryan notes that assuming that knights carry money in chivalric romances seems problematic and out of keeping with the imagined world (53). (I discuss the implications of this observation in greater detail and argue for the importance of our understanding of the rules of how to build and use such imagined worlds in chapter 5.) Zoran's account of total space fails to account for a similar limitation: by making all spatial information relevant to the total space of the narrative, the term itself is unable to account for the way that our knowledge of real space might be rendered less relevant in particular narrative works. As he says, "It is impossible to imagine space as anything other than total" (329).

It is precisely the constructedness of narrative space that Zoran overlooks when talking about it at the level of total space. By *constructedness* I am trying to distinguish how we build cognitive maps of spaces in everyday life, or through the kinds of linguistic references that Zoran emphasizes, from the often artificial ways that artistic media can use space. If we turn back to Ronen we can see the way that her language of framing spaces emphasizes that individual texts can construct their space by bounding it. Ronen is essentially focusing on what Zoran would call the topographical understanding of narrative space—the space as we are able to reconstruct it over the course of reading, rather than the way that we perceive that space over time or how it makes certain kinds of movements possible. The advantage of Ronen's approach is that she places greater emphasis on what we could describe as the "staging" of space—the way that a particular scene is created with surrounding spaces. The case of theater makes the importance of such staging choices obvious, since it depends on the fundamental ontological distinction between those spaces that will appear on stage and those that are merely implied by the backdrop scenery, or mentioned in dialog. This staging is an artistic decision that colors the entire production and is frequently technical at its base: the set designer has to tackle fundamental questions about how to move characters on and off the stage. Especially when the production involves effects that depart from our mundane life—creatures who fly, spaces that collapse, a staged execution—set design will significantly be dictated by technical possibilities. The audience for theatrical staging is intuitively aware of the distinction between stage and background space. Some theatrical productions may make a seemingly inaccessible space occupied—most obviously when a production moves out into the audience and what initially seems like spectator space becomes part of the staged fictional world—but in most cases audiences maintain a firm understanding of the line between scenery and stage space. Such playful violations are effective precisely because the audience has such a clear understanding of how this distinction normally works. Although Ronen herself does not discuss theatrical space, her contrast between the foreground setting and the surrounding, framing spaces makes her theory open to the construction of these kinds of artificially bounded spaces. Just as important, this framing is a positive, intentional component of the aesthetic design that continues as the work moves through particular scenes and their implied space, rather than simply being a general lack of information about spaces. To return to the language that I have developed from digital narrative, theater provides a clear case of the way that the primary space of action is framed by an orienting space from which that is viewed.

More recent cognitive work on narrative space, which likewise emphasizes the continuities between our perception of everyday and narrative space, repeats many of the strengths and limitations that we have noted in Zoran's theory. As David Herman explains in *Story Logic,* "Narratives can also be thought of as systems of verbal or visual cues prompting their readers to *spatialize* storyworlds into evolving configurations of participants, objects, and places"[2] (263). Herman's account is especially powerful for building on Zoran's insight that narrative spaces must be understood (in part) through what he describes as their chronotopic basis: how agents move through space in the course of the story. In particular, Herman emphasizes that spaces are marked by actual and potential passages: "Building on the distinction between figure and ground, Barbara Landau and Ray Jackendoff have redescribed places as *regions* occupied by *landmarks* or reference objects, and *paths* as the routes one travels to get from place to place" (277–8). This example of paths and landmarks makes clear that starting from natural language narrative provides a cognitive model that emphasizes the continuities between our perception of space in a story and our perception of space in our everyday lives. Such a cognitive approach recognizes that people build models of space all the time when they are told an anecdote or even given directions. But this focus on the continuities between everyday and literary space gives little attention to the artificiality of some artistic spaces, and thus repeats the problem that Zoran encounters when he explains the nature of "total space." Herman describes the way that stories help listeners or readers to "relocate from the HERE and NOW of the act of narration to other space-time coordinates" and to "transport themselves" into these new spaces (271). The pleasure that we might take in an awareness of the constructedness of space (the way that the production designers are using conventional features in theater, for example) is not accounted for well by a theory that emphasizes the continuities between cognitive mapping in everyday experiences and the reading of narrative.

We can see the problems with, and a solution to, this disregard for the boundedness of narrative space by turning to a critic invoked by both Herman

---

2. As with other chapters, any emphasis in quotes is from the original text, unless otherwise noted.

and Zoran in their search to define space in part through real and potential temporal movement—Mikhail Bakhtin. Zoran and Herman both make clear that it is by means of the temporal unfolding of the narrative that we build up a model of the seemingly atemporal topographical space. Bakhtin's fusion of space and time is an essential supplement to Ronen's simpler model of framing, and, as I will show, helps us to discuss what it means to observe a narrative space from some outside place. Bakhtin's familiar examples of literary chronotopes have provided concrete and intuitive models for how we can talk about "the intrinsic connectedness of temporal and spatial relationships that are artistically expressed in literature" (84). Bakhtin's description of the "adventure-time" central to the Greek adventure novel is especially well known. The space of the adventure novel is essentially "abstract" (99) and is defined entirely by the contingency of the events and meetings that occur there: "In order for the adventure to develop it needs space, and plenty of it. The contingency that governs events is inseparably tied up with space, measured primarily by *distance* on the one hand and by *proximity* on the other (and varying degrees of both)" (99). Such spaces are interchangeable (100) and exist only to make possible abrupt events that occur "suddenly" (92) and by chance. Because these events must be random and abrupt, adventure time is fundamentally severed from the everyday time and space that gives order to ordinary life.

We have already seen that Zoran makes rather loose use of the chronotope. In part this is because, as Gary Saul Morson and Caryl Emerson note, Bakhtin "never offers a concise definition" of the chronotope; instead "he first offers some initial comments, and then repeatedly alternates concrete examples with further generalizations. In the course of this exposition, the term turns out to have several related meanings" (366–7). Especially crucial is the issue raised by Herman about the degree to which it can be applied to everyday, rather than only literary, spaces. Among Bakhtin's best analysts, Michael Holquist has associated the chronotope with extraliterary space. With Katerina Clark he describes the chronotope as "a bridge, not a wall" between the actual world and the literary world (279). In *Dialogism,* Holquist is even more explicit: "As a category in dialogism, the chronotope is grounded in simultaneity at *all* levels, including those of both 'literature' and 'real life'" (115). Bernhard Scholz offers a contrary reading of the text/world relation in the chronotope by turning to the Kantian thought that provided the framework for Bakhtin's work, paying particular attention to Bakhtin's footnote regarding Kant. Bakhtin writes, "Here we employ the Kantian evaluation of the importance of these forms [of space and time] in the cognitive process, but differ from Kant in taking them not as 'transcendental' but as forms of the most immediate reality. We shall attempt to show the role these forms play in the process of concrete artistic cognition" (150; citing 85). For Scholz, the central puzzle to Bakhtin's chronotope in this Kantian context is the equation of cognition and representation. Kant "would have found it problematic, if not impossible, to follow Bakhtin and place representations on a par with perceptions, if by representations are meant perceptions and/or thoughts encoded by means of one or another symbolic system" (150).

This insight leads Scholz to pay attention to a puzzling and frequently overlooked remark by Bakhtin: "The relationships themselves that exist *among* chronotopes cannot enter into any of the relationships contained *within* chronotopes" (154, citing 252). Scholz proposes an important distinction between the perspective within and outside of the chronotope: the critic "can focus on the manner in which the sequential and the appositional ordering of the manifold of appearances of a particular chronotope appears to the personages populating the world ordered by that chronotope, or s/he can focus on the manner in which that ordering appears 'as an entity,' i.e. looked at from the outside" (155). He gives the example of the Greek adventure novel:

> Looked at from the inside, all appears to be governed by chance through and through: Bakhtin speaks of a "veritable downpour of 'suddenlys' and 'at just that moments.'" However, looked at from the outside, i.e. from the perspective of the reader, sameness and unchangingness reign supreme, and the eventual "happy ending" is never in doubt. (155)

Scholz summarizes this distinction between "the external perspective on chronotopes (understanding them as the constituent categories of literature), rather than the internal perspective (understanding them as forms of cognition)" (156). Scholz makes clear that the chronotope does not simply extend from real world to representations in the literary work, but is instead a construction whose relationship to the larger world in which it is deployed must be considered carefully. Although Scholz would be sympathetic to the idea, articulated by Holquist and Clark, that the chronotope is relevant both to the world represented in the narrative and to the everyday world in which we read and study that narrative, he implies that calling this a "bridge" is problematic. The experience of space and time inside the narrative (by characters) and outside the narrative (as readers) are two entirely separate constructions, and failing to recognize this distinction means misunderstanding the relevance of the chronotope to our role as critic and reader.

I find Scholz's interpretation of Bakhtin especially powerful because it allows us to recognize a limitation that we have seen in the other accounts of space that I have discussed above: the problems of dealing with intentionally bounded spaces, such as those that we see in theater. If Scholz is right in emphasizing the fundamental distinction between our position inside and outside of the narrative chronotope, then we have a powerful tool for interpreting how spaces are constructed in these ways. In particular, Scholz helps us to talk about something that has only been hinted at by scholars like Ronen, Zoran, and Herman: how this external position orients us to these represented spaces, and allows us to *do things* with them as readers and critics.

ORIENTING SPACES IN DIGITAL AND PRINT NARRATIVE

Let us return, then, to digital narrative and the important distinction between primary and orienting spaces. This distinction captures a self-consciously artificial dimension of narrative space that is rarely given much attention in narrative theory. The theory that comes closest to what we see in digital narrative is the frequently overlooked contrast between the interior and exterior perspective on the chronotope that Scholz reveals in Bakhtin.

In particular, Scholz suggests that our external perspective on the chronotopes within a story allows us to do different things with the story, to define "the constituent categories of literature." In digital narratives this external orientation and use of individual primary spaces is quite explicit. Games may also use the external perspective on their individual spaces as a way to offer a range of options or choices to players, with the larger (orienting) space of the gameworld providing a perspective on the variations within individual landscapes and their particular gameplay challenges. This kind of larger space is especially important in games based on spaces defined externally to the individual narrative. For example, in a game based on the *Lord of the Rings* novels, or the *Star Wars* films, players have a sense of the larger universe in which these individual play spaces are set, and may look forward to getting to "visit" Mordor or Tatooine and contrast them with their own expectations based on the cross-media narrative world. Games like this can help to flesh out a narrative world—but do so by invoking a perspective external to the individual chronotope encountered within the primary space. Within individual primary spaces, our experience of these games can be quite different. A game that might have a strong narrative focus or whimsical quality at the external level of orienting spaces can be frantic and disorienting once the player is within the primary space of play. Likewise, the player's motivation to return to these primary spaces might be inconsistent with the design of the playable space itself. For example, within the playable space the player might be forced to survive a desperate life-or-death battle, but choose to return to this space from the orienting space of the game menu to replay the mission for comparatively trivial reasons—such as earning a player trophy. I have already argued that the issue of the use of narrative elements is an important unifying theme in digital storytelling, and one that draws our attention to this neglected issue in other media. The fact that game space leads us to Scholz's distinction between interior and exterior perspectives on the chronotope is typical of how digital narrative can help us to put greater emphasis on our use of the story and its elements even in non-digital stories.

Let us turn to J. R. Carpenter's 2008 *In Absentia* as an example of a work that explores thematically this kind of dual space in a digital narrative. Carpenter describes the Mile End neighborhood of Montreal, with a particular focus on community development and gentrification. The work takes the form of a map using the Google Maps API (Application Programming Interface). Users can pan or zoom the map (as they can in any instance of Google Maps). Onto this space Carpenter has inserted images marking particular locations, such as a chair, a fire hydrant, or words such as "Logement à Louer" or "Fermé." Each of these location markers can be selected, and will launch text in an inset window (see figure 2.8). Some of this text tells anecdotes ("I run into my neighbour on the street and he asks me if I've noticed the stranger who has 'moved in.' My neighbour is worried that the man has come up from New York for retribution [. . .].") as well as other sorts of found texts, such as an advertisement for a roommate ("hey friends. my roommate was just offered the best one person apartment ever [. . .] very cheap, totally beautiful,

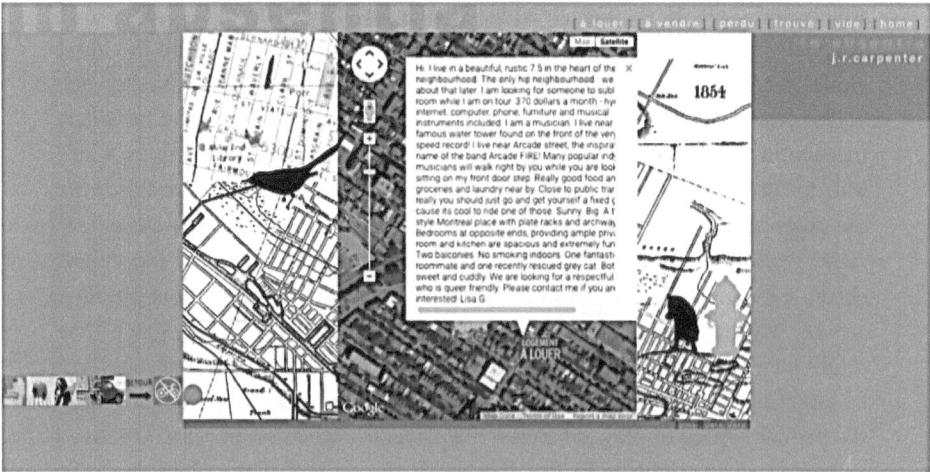

FIGURE 2.8. J. R. Carpenter, *In Absentia*

good landlord, fantastic neighbours [. . .]") or texts authored by others, such as Lance Blombren and Daniel Canty. All of these texts describe finding, renting, and owning city space.

Google Maps functions as a kind of secondary space, external to the stories told and often at odds with that space. While the inserted texts are decidedly individual (each is tagged to its author, Carpenter or others) Google provides a more abstract orientation to space. Where the orientation space provided by commercial video games is usually superior to that of playable space—giving the player a sense of the overall arc of the game—it is not clear that Google provides the best way to view city space in *In Absentia*. In the real world, Google is a tool used to accomplish certain things—particularly navigation and pragmatic orientation—even as we understand its limitations and inaccuracies. In a gameworld—or, indeed, any fictional world—other than internal consistency there is no way to evaluate the orienting space of the game, and thus little opportunity to ask whether that space is accurate or appropriate.³ It seems that it is precisely the intimate and individual quality of the textually described spaces that Carpenter values. She tells this story in the "perdu" section:

> We throw the orange ball and our dog brings it back to us. We throw the orange ball and our dog brings it back. We throw the orange ball and he chases and sometimes we miss. Eight-and-a-half years we've been walking up and down this alleyway and it's hard to say how many orange balls we've sent sailing over cinder block fences into thigh-high tomatoes or sunk into knee-deep snow. Sorry if we've ever snuck into your yard in an attempt to retrieve the lost ball de jour. Dogs know nothing of private property.

This anecdote emphasizes things that have no place in a Google Map: the repetitious pathways, the "cinder block fences" too small to show up as a mapped feature, the motions of dogs that "know nothing of private property" and thus ignore precisely the sorts of boundaries that such maps reinforce. Although these anecdotes seem to resist the city map locating each precisely, it is clear that Google Maps is the precondition for telling these stories: the

---

3. This is not to say that players might not critique the orienting space in pragmatic terms by complaining that certain spaces in the fictional world have no playable missions, or guess where a future game expansion might fit within this space. And, of course, there are many attempts to map such fictional spaces using Google Maps, such as this map of Middle Earth: https://imgur.com/gallery/whKZ7KM/new. But such maps, created after the fact, have the same partial relationship to these fictional spaces that maps have to the real world.

map provides a way of holding together and giving shape to these individual experiences.

If we return to the other three theories of space that I discussed in the previous section of this chapter, Ronen's account of frames organized around a central "scene" provides the most obvious model for the kinds of spaces that we see in digital narrative; her account also resonates with Bakhtin's contrast between the interior and exterior perspectives on the chronotope. But, as Scholz suggests, our position outside of the represented chronotope is much more radically heterogeneous than the framing that Ronen describes. Carpenter makes this heterogeneity the focus of her work, emphasizing the fundamental disconnection between a high-level commercial mapping of city space and the experience of individual locations within the neighborhood. For the dog chasing a ball over walls and through gardens, the experience of the neighborhood is defined less by boundaries and efficient directions, and more by repetition, meandering, and the transient conditions of the space (snow, gardens) that Google cannot map. Likewise, when a literary critic observes a chronotope from the outside while doing interpretation or history, he or she is not inside the chronotope as a space to be occupied, but is instead treating it as an object. This secondary space often has a utilitarian relationship to the playable space—just like the external prospective on the chronotope allows the literary critic to treat it as an object of analysis. Although we have seen that the distinction between primary and orienting space has a fundamental role in digital narratives of all forms, Carpenter unpacks the ideological implications of this distinction, to which critics should be sensitive while analyzing a narrative. From this perspective, what Zoran misses in his otherwise excellent essay is precisely that total space is defined by a bounding space from which we observe the text, the "somewhere" of reading, and that this space is not continuous with the space embodied in the work.

Obviously, print narrative does not usually stage this "somewhere," this orienting space, as a literal part of the work in the way that most digital narrative does. And the recent cognitive focus in narrative theory probably makes it even harder to recognize the role of this orientation, since that work has tended to emphasize how readers make sense of the text rather than the way that the text functions as an object to be acted upon. The key quality of the dual space model I have offered here is that attending to this orienting space invites readers to do different things with the primary spaces of the story. This is a crucial quality of digital narrative: because readers of such texts usually need to do something to get the full meaning of the work, they need to be given much more explicit guidance on how to manipulate the work. Carpenter's decision to associate orienting space with the corporate mapping of urban space makes clear that the manipulation of these narrative spaces is not aesthetically or politically neutral. There are some physical manifestations of this kind of orienting space in print. We might think of a textbook in which individual stories are surrounded by some other institutional framework that quizzes students on the narratives, prompts writing through "discussion questions," or even uses these narratives as examples for the sake of learning a foreign language or diagnosing a mental disorder. In these cases, whatever chronotope that exists within the story would not only be fundamentally different from the chronotope of the textbook, but the latter would invite readers to treat the inset stories as objects that are to be used for a purpose.

Recent work on "distant reading" can be seen as another way of constructing an entirely different, external chronotope from which the print text is examined. Franco Moretti provides a good example of how these kinds of secondary, orienting spaces might be discussed even in much more traditional print narratives. In *Graphs, Maps, Trees* Moretti discusses Mary Mitford's *Our Village* at some length. Mitford attracts Moretti's attention because her individual stories of village life imply a larger map of spaces, which Moretti then sketches: "[. . .] You make a map of the book, and everything changes. The twenty-four stories of Mitford's first volume [. . .] arrange themselves in a little solar system, with the village at the centre of the pattern, and two roughly concentric rings around it" (36–7). This map is not contained anywhere within the book, and in fact contrasts to the narrative space: "the road 'from B— to S—,' so present at the beginning of the book, has disappeared. narrative space is not linear here, it is *circular*" (37). It is for this reason that Moretti posits his mapping technique as something preliminary for analysis rather than as an inherent part of the experience of the text: "They are a good way to prepare a text for analysis. [. . .] And with a little luck, these maps will be *more than the sum of their parts*: they will possess 'emerging' qualities, which were not visible at the lower level" (53). It is easy to see Moretti's mapping as a way of doing things with texts that echoes Bakhtin's "external" perspective on the chronotope occupied by critics and historians. These maps are an especially good example of the way that a story can imply a secondary, orienting space that is contained nowhere within the text. Readers are invited to treat the individual spaces as forming some larger whole that is outside of those characters' experience.

Moretti is encouraging critics to create a literal map as a kind of secondary space during analysis, but there are other ways in which narratives can imply an analytic space outside the text in a more metaphorical way. This kind of perspective, where the reader is invited to imagine a space and perform a kind of analysis of which the narrator may be unaware, is an understudied part of narrative. It is a superior, analytic perspective implied when George Eliot in *Middlemarch* and Henry James in "Daisy Miller" subtitle their stories "a study." Indeed, the difference between the ways that these two narratives function as "studies" suggests the variety of ways in which the reader can be positioned externally to the fictional world. While James problematizes the way that Daisy has been treated as an object and type and thus complicates our objective position, Eliot's "study in provincial life" is a somewhat more straightforward description of setting designed to provide a context for interpreting the problems and behavior of her characters. This same work of the reader is invoked by graphic novelist Chris Ware in *Building Stories*, a narrative that takes the form of a box of differently printed storytelling forms, including a bound book that echoes the "Little Golden" books for children, a hard board that invokes board games, and graphic narratives printed in many different sizes and orientations. Ware provides little guidance about the order or priority of reading, and the reader, instead, is being invited to build the story in the playful way we associate with toys. Indeed, he has imposed on the reader of his stories a very literal orientating space in the board game box, which requires a very different form of interaction—unpacking the whole, spreading out the larger items on the floor or table, and taking inventory of the materials in much the same way that we would at the start of a game. Obviously, the examples of Moretti, Ware, and Eliot and James are spatial in very different ways—some literal, some metaphorical—but all of them draw our attention to the way that the reader is occupying a position external to the events of the story and being asked to read these spaces as something to be analyzed or manipulated. To return to Bakhtin, this location is external to the space and time as experienced by the characters, and thus entirely different chronotopically.

MEDIA ARCHAEOLOGY, AGAIN

I hope to have shown that digital narrative reveals a complexity in our sense of space that is muted in traditional print stories. As Moretti's example of a village space suggests, this will give us a new way to talk about how stories ask readers to engage with texts. This chapter has performed the same move as the previous one: we have seen that digital media allows us to grasp features of a common narrative element (space) that are harder to see in other media like print and film.

In these first two chapters I have described two theoretical absences in narrative theories based (primarily) on print stories: the intrigue and the orienting space. Making these theoretical gaps visible is my goal in this book, and it should make clear what I meant in the Introduction when I describe this project as a work of narratological archaeology. The design of the book and the way that we are directed to use it is a quality that is relatively marginal in most forms of storytelling, but once we recognize our role as intriguee in digital narrative, we can see how other media can sometimes create an interface for user actions. Likewise, we can see that print texts often do create an orienting space in which readers are asked to do something with the individual elements of the stories told. In both of these chapters we have seen that viewing theoretical concepts through digital narrative reveals tensions and ambiguities within this term. This chapter has also showed how the framework provided by digital narrative can clarify our interpretation of theoretical statements directly. I have shown that interpreters brought to the chronotope a bias that lead to a subtle misreading of this concept. Although Bakhtin is, of course, coming out of a print tradition, our expectations about how space operates in print led critics to misread him and largely overlook the crucial distinction between the chronotope as it is seen inside and outside the text. In other words, the reading that I have done in this chapter informs not just narrative practice but also the history and interpretation of our terms for narrative study themselves.

Finally, these two chapters resonate with each other by drawing our attention to the way that readers (or players) are invited to *use* the work. Games frequently depend on the tension between the events in the primary space of the story, and those that occur in the orienting space that provides a context for using that primary space: replaying a harrowing mission in a shooter in order to earn an achievement award, for example. This kind of use is often not as obvious in the novel, but Moretti reminds us that we can use books and their component elements in a lot of different ways. One goal of this book, then, is to understand narrative as an object with a user interface that invites certain kinds of uses, and to consider the implications of this fact for narrative theory. In fact, we will turn to the user interface directly in the next chapter.

CHAPTER 3

UI Time and the Digital Event

MY FIRST two chapters have focused on two very different kinds of narrative concepts. The issue of narration and the implied author represents a core subject of debate within narrative theory, one that has resulted in complex and well-established terms for the entities that are taken to have told and received the story. Setting, conversely, is a perennial topic that nonetheless has never quite cohered into broadly accepted terms and models in the way that narration has. I would like to turn now to what is arguably the central element of narrative: time and the event. Although the distinction between the time of narrative events (story/fabula) and the time of their telling by a narrator (discourse/sjuzhet) has been debated over the last forty years, it remains a fundamental feature of narrative theory. In this chapter, I will argue that digital narrative introduces a third form of time at the level of the user's interaction with the story that is distinct from both. Although this user interface (UI) time is largely invisible in other media, it does raise some interesting issues about the way that the reader or viewer encounters the material text in other forms of storytelling.

This chapter will also dive more deeply into the technical construction of computing devices and away from the somewhat more general concepts of interface elements and the common features of video games, which were the focus of the previous chapter. As is appropriate regarding such a central but philosophical topic like the event, this chapter will investigate how software exists temporally in general.

TIME AND THE EVENT

"Simply put," writes Porter Abbott at the outset of *The Cambridge Introduction to Narrative*, "narrative is *the representation of an event or a series of events*"[1] (13). Narrative theory has long recognized that developing an understanding of what makes something *an event* is crucial to defining narrative itself. In her introduction to *Narrative across Media,* Marie-Laure Ryan offers a definition of narrativity based on three conditions: it must create a world with characters and objects; the world must undergo changes; and those changes must be based on causality and motivations in a way that allows for interpretation (8–9).[2]

The way that events are represented in the narrative is central to how the story constructs time. At the outset of *Narratology* Mieke Bal defines the event and some supporting terms this way:

> A *narrative text* is a text in which an agent relates ("tells") a story in a particular medium, such as language, imagery, sound, buildings, or a combination thereof. A *story* is a fabula that is presented in a certain manner. A *fabula* is a series of logically and chronologically related events that are caused or experienced by actors. An *event* is the transition from one state to another state. *Actors* are agents that perform actions. They are not necessarily human. *To act* is defined here as to cause or to experience an event. (5)

A significant amount of energy in narrative theory over the last three decades has been generated by the relationship between the fabula events and the way that they are presented in what Bal calls the story. The distinction between fabula and story has been articulated by other critics using confusingly different terms: fabula vs. sjuzhet, histoire vs. récit, story vs. discourse, and so on. In *Fictions of Discourse* (1994) Patrick O'Neill provides a helpful overview

---

1. As with other chapters, any emphasis in quotes is from the original text, unless otherwise noted.

2. It is worth recognizing the recent philosophical and cultural interest in retheorizing the event, even though that falls outside of narrative theory. Alain Badiou is best known for theorizing the event as fundamentally disrupting our current ways of thinking about the world and its possibilities. Back in 1994 Gary Saul Morson made a particularly strong argument against models of time and plot that make events seem inevitable before turning to Bakhtin's notion of "sideshadows."

of these terminological variations, and shows how fundamental the distinction between story events and their telling in discourse is across a wide variety of narrative theories—from Aristotle through Michael Toolan (21)—and goes on to argue that this relationship is the basis for a certain kind of narrative game: "There is clearly a sense in which all narratives are a form of semiotic game, presenting particular and particularly effective arrangements and interrelationships of real or invented events for reception and interpretation by known and/or unknown audiences" (26). For consistency's sake, I will adopt Seymour Chatman's widely used terms in the remainder of this chapter: *story* is the events in their causal, temporal order, and *discourse* is the way that those events are presented to the reader through the particular narration of a storyteller.

An influential intervention in this theory was Gérard Genette's *Narrative Discourse* (1972), which provided a systematic framework for several crucial elements of the relationship between the events of the story and discourse. Of particular significance was Genette's emphasis on order, duration, and frequency of events. Genette provided technical language for what we would more casually refer to as flashbacks (analepsis) and foreshadowing (prolepsis). His work also called attention to what we can describe as the speed of the story: how some events are skipped over entirely, others are presented as a general summary, while others are described at much greater length than their real-life temporal duration would warrant. Bal formalized Genette's analysis as a system for discussing two kinds of time: the real-life time of the story events and the time that they take up within the discourse of their telling. When events pass quickly with little narrative details, Bal describes these as summary, and when the time of the story slows down or event stops to allow extensive description, Bal calls this a slow-down or pause. There has been some debate about these terms,[3] but in general Genette's framework, supplemented by Bal's terminology, has proven to be quite durable over the last thirty years.

ACCOUNTING FOR THE INTERFACE

The identification of causally interpretable and narratively significant events and an appreciation of how those events are ordered and presented to the audience has, then, been a fundamental part of narrative theory since its

---

3. See, for example, Hilary Dannenberg's discussion of "temporal orchestration" (50) as an alternative model in *Coincidence and Counterfactuality*.

inception. We can recognize that these issues of order and speed apply equally well to many narrative forms—from print novels to films and graphic narrative. Is there something unique about the event and time in digital narrative?

The question of whether the events that make up a digital narrative are different from those in other media was a point of debate in early criticism. The first wave of scholarship celebrating the potential of digital narrative often made exaggerated claims about the way that it would change the nature of narrative events. Some critics suggested that the reader would become the co-creator of the story by choosing some actions or following some story pathways rather than others. At the core of this way of thinking about digital narrative was the frequently invoked analog example of the Choose Your Own Adventure novels in which readers face certain decision points by the character, where they are asked to turn to a particular page to continue reading based on their choices. This kind of variability of events is what Marie-Laure Ryan calls ontological interactivity. Ryan distinguishes between exploratory and ontological interactivity: "In the *exploratory* mode, users navigate the display, but this activity does not make the fictional history nor does it alter the plot: users have no impact on the destiny of the virtual world. In the *ontological* mode, by contrast, the decisions of the user send the history of the virtual world on different forking paths" (*Avatars* 108). Exploratory interactivity is most common in early hypertexts, where the reader is generally encountering a preexisting story in variable ways, reading different lexia in different orders. Such narratives generally do not prompt the storytelling challenges of ontological interactivity, since the whole text can be constructed around definite events. Ontological works, conversely, pose greater challenges for creating coherent events and a sense of narrative progression.

Espen Aarseth's 1997 *Cybertext* challenged many of the myths and vague assertions that had grown up around digital media, including the idea that these reader-selected events made digital narratives different from linear storytelling. In response to the claim that digital narratives are somehow nonlinear, he remarks: "How can any text be linear? Clearly, the physical properties of the codex are not enough to ensure it, as so many paper experiments have shown. Furthermore, any book can be opened at any page and can be started at any point. The book form, then, is intrinsically neither linear nor nonlinear but, more precisely, random access (to borrow from computer technology)" (46). Likewise, he notes that the concept of interactive fiction is "used repeatedly without clarification" and considers two possible explanations for why: "Either it means nothing in particular or its meaning is perceived to be so trivial that it is self-explanatory" (50). Aarseth's critique of the uncritical celebration of interactivity as a kind of audience freedom can apply to analog as well as digital media. For all that Choose Your Own Adventure novels seem "present" and open to multiple possibilities, those possibilities are created and structured by an author ahead of time before the reader ever encounters them. These stories are fundamentally similar to traditional retrospective narration, even if our interface on those possible stories creates a greater feeling of choice and the present. In other words, Aarseth argues that we should see the *story* experienced through digital media as not fundamentally different from other media. This is why, in part, he sees the role of narrative in games as far less interesting than their ludic possibilities. Because the events of the narrative in these digital narratives could be fundamentally different from one reading or playing to the next (at least in cases of ontological interactivity), critics have continued to try to characterize their difference from other media. In *The Possible Worlds of Hypertext Fiction* (2010), Alice Bell raises "The Question of Uniqueness" in hypertext fiction by noting that some of the techniques used here share a metaleptic, alienating effect with other postmodernist print texts: "As the superficial associations between Storyspace hypertext narratives and some types of print fiction imply, hypertext may not necessarily offer new narrative devices. It does, however, offer authors an alternative context in which to place them" (19).

In his recent book, *Transmedial Narratology and Contemporary Media Culture,* Jan-Noël Thon tries to strike a balance between the way our experience of narrative is the same across media, and the importance of recognizing the specific features of the medium through which that narrative is encountered:

> The application of medium-specific charity that allows recipients to cope with some of the more complex and indirect forms of representational correspondence to be found in verbal and pictorial as well as in audiovisual, verbal-pictorial, and interactive modes of representation has turned out to be particularly salient with regard to the representation of local situations, while the ways in which these situations are located within the global storyworld as a whole by establishing spatial, temporal, causal, and ontological relations between them appears to be generally more transmedial, as recipients here primarily take their cues from what is being represented as opposed to medium-specific elements of representation. (121)

If we apply this careful articulation to Aarseth's 1997 claim, we can say that the work that we do to comprehend narrative events and to organize them into a story (separate from the discourse in which they are encountered) is relatively medium independent. In other words, digital events are not fundamentally different in nature from the narrative events encountered through other media.

If we want to understand what is distinctive about time and the digital event, then, we need to look not so much at the way that we (re)construct causality and change, but instead at the context in which we encounter those events. At this point it would be helpful to move from generalizations about digital narratives to a particular example. Let us consider Jason Nelson's *Game, Game, Game, and Again Game,* which imitates a traditional two-dimensional "platformer" that asks the player to move an avatar (a small, spider-like scribble) across the screen to reveal text and move on to the next "level" (see figure 3.1).

This work is an especially good example of the way that time and events are handled in digital media because it so explicitly draws on and repurposes conventional features of video games. Indeed, as the title suggests, this is a game about how and why we play games and how those games connect to our sense of meaning and progression. As Lori Emerson puts it in *Reading Writing Interfaces,* this work "deliberately undoes video game conventions (of accumu-

FIGURE 3.1. Jason Nelson, *Game, Game, Game, and Again Game*

lation, progress, winning/losing, clear moral victories, immersion) through a nonsensical point system and mechanisms" (40).[4] Nelson's work exemplifies many common qualities of the event and time in digital texts. Obviously, the game implies a causal dynamic: the player is engaged in a story about progression and antagonism, with some clear pitfalls to be avoided (the blue squiggle) and the door-like goal that the player will try to reach. In many ways, Nelson turns the conventions of video games on their head, since the player often has to take a route that seems counterintuitive—in this case, plunging towards the sun at the bottom of the screen, which prompts a pathway to the door to appear at the last moment. Even though we encounter this story in a different context (emerging as it does, from our gameplay actions) it clearly draws on all of our conventional—and, as Thon might say, transmedial—understanding of action, cause, consequence, and time.

Is there something different about the event and time in this work than we might encounter in a print text? Let me begin with a very simple observation about time: in addition to our actions as the player in moving the avatar and experiencing the consequences, time is clearly passing, and elements on the screen happen regardless of whether we act or not. Objects flash and spin, the blue squiggle that is our antagonist moves in what turns out to be a loop, and the whole screen flickers from time to time in a glitch-like way. The game has a kind of aliveness and time that are separate from the events that we cause through our actions, and separate as well from any kind of reconstructed story that we might discover in the process of exploring this world. This time represents the "context" in which we encounter the generally transmedial story, and thus it will be the focus for most of the remainder of this chapter.

I will call this User Interface (or UI) time, drawing on but also repurposing a term first coined by Marjorie Luesebrink in 1998 but expanded and systematized by Raine Koskimaa. Luesebrink uses the term as a contrast with cognitive time to distinguish the mechanical time of interacting with a device from the time represented in the work ("Hypertext Fiction in the Twilight Zone"). Koskimaa extends this distinction to cover four kinds of time. John David Zuern provides a concise summary of Koskimaa's model:

> Koskimaa's *user time* represents the time individual users spend engaging with the work. *Discourse time* is the time the work itself takes to deliver its content to the user, for example, the length of a text or a running time of a film. *Story time* designates the temporality represented in the work itself

---

4. See also Astrid Ensslin's discussion of the "Flash-platform poetry game tetralogy *ArcticAcre: Odditites and Curious Lands*" to which this work belongs (129).

[. . .]. *System time,* according to Koskimaa, is "The time of the cybertext system states" [. . .]. This category can be understood to include the time it takes a computational device to process the work's code, which can vary substantially from computer to computer, and, in the case of Internet-based works, the time it takes the data composing the artwork to travel from a server to the user's display device. (482–3; citing Koskimaa, "Approaches" 136)

Koskimaa's emphasis in this account falls largely on a measurement of duration, but I want to treat UI time as a somewhat more flexible concept that describes the relationship between stasis, progression, and repetition in order to bring it into line with the story/discourse distinction. In the case of Nelson's game, we can progress relatively quickly to the next screen simply by rolling our avatar forward, and allowing it to drop into this pit and then opening up our pathway to the door at the bottom right. But there is a great deal of what Genette might call iterative temporality here as the arrows spin and the blue squiggle that is our antagonist moves in a fixed circuit. UI time as I will describe it tries to capture the aesthetic dimensions of the design of the interface's time, and how those resonate with the other elements of a digital narrative's temporality.

PLACING UI TIME IN NARRATIVE MODELS

As I noted at the outset, narrative theory has long distinguished between the time represented in the story and the time of the telling of the narrative, or its discourse. It has also been widely applied to film and graphic narrative, and others have made the case that it can apply to still images as well. I will argue that the UI time that I have been describing in this chapter cannot be accommodated within this model.

Let us return to an unproblematic example of digital narrative that I already discussed in chapter 1: a hypertext work in the Storyspace model. In Michael Joyce's *afternoon* we clearly see a distinction between the story events and the voices that narrate them. Our main character Peter witnesses a car crash, and interacts with many other characters including his ex-wife Lisa and his boss Wert. We learn about these events from different narrators—primarily from Peter, but also from the therapist Lolly and another character, Nausicaa—and through overlapping scenes and passages. The reader can choose to follow different links to access different parts of the story, but the narration itself in any given section looks like traditional literary text. In this regard, *afternoon* provides a straightforward example of the story/discourse distinction. This should be no surprise, since as an early example of an emerging new medium, *afternoon* naturally embodies traditional narrative models familiar from print. We have, then, two very traditional forms of time in this work: the story that we reconstruct about Peter, his wife, and his son, and the time of narration, which we encounter in the voices of various speakers and in a somewhat variable order that is shaped by the choices that the reader makes in navigating the work.

Given these two times, how do we theorize the temporality of the UI? Let us recognize that this is an important variable in the aesthetic design of the work. If, for example, the story did not remain idle but instead moved forward without user choice, the experience of the work would be very different. The film-like works of Young-Hae Chang Heavy Industries, for example, involve phrases, words, or parts of words flashing onto a relatively plain background, timed to the beats of always heavily rhythmic music. These works have an ongoing, sometimes rushing temporality and rhythm that are very different from the UI time constructed in the infinitely patient Storyspace system. Of course, this is not an either–or situation; many digital texts create different degrees of UI time integrated with some periods of idleness. Let us take the example of a minor change to the reading experience: the way that the *Born Magazine* collaborative poems use the transitions between lines of text to control the speed of reading. I have already discussed *Outrances* in chapter 1, and that work clearly segments the pace of reading in a way relevant to UI time. Other works produced for *Born* engage with the time of reading in very different ways. In *House Fire,* the opening line of the poem, "Here is a Girl" appears on the screen, and shortly after a line drawing of a young woman fades in. After a short delay, the next line, "with a house in her eyes," appears and then, after another delay, a next line: "or, what is left of it, the house no longer a house." The poem has moments where the forward motion pauses, waiting for a user mouse-click, and others where the text is revealed at a computer-controlled pace. Essentially a work like this presents a traditional poem but controls the pace at which the individual lines can be read—slowing down reading and introducing a system of segmentation that supplements the poetic line. A work like this represents a balance between Young-Hae Chang Heavy Industries's complete control of the time of reading and the stasis of a work like *afternoon*.

House Fire, then, introduces a subtly different sense of time in making the reader wait for these transitions. Or consider works that require what Aarseth calls "non-trivial" effort on the part of the reader to make the text visible, such as three-dimensional poetry where users must manipulate the perspective to be able to read the text. A good example of a relatively early electronic narrative that involves user action framed in an explicitly temporal way is Ingrid Ankerson and Megan Sapnar's *Cruising* (2001). The work takes the form of a strip of images connected in a film-like way, one after another, with the text of the work written continuously above those images, evoking the way that sprocket holes are placed in film. The strip of images and words can move slowly or quickly left or right, depending on the mouse position side to side; likewise, our perspective on them can be zoomed in or out based on the mouse position up or down (see figure 3.2).

In effect, reading the story and viewing the images involves finding the right position for the mouse where the text is both large enough and moving slowly enough to be read. Indeed, *Cruising* is a great example of UI time because the temporality of our interaction with the work clearly resonates with the aesthetic design of the whole text. Ankerson and Sapnar's work describes an adolescent past of cruising around a small Wisconsin town narrated from the point of view of someone older; the final line "eying life through a car we couldn't yet take to the world" clearly shows the contrasting perspectives of the younger narrated characters and the older narrator. The UI dynamic of the work, where the user must strike the right balance between the closeness and distance of the point of view, as well as the appropriate passage of time, exactly matches this thematic interest in the tension between a present and past self. This example clearly shows that UI time is a distinct aesthetic level to the work, and that digital narratives have to organize this tripartite structure: story, narration, and interface.

EVENTS IN PROGRAMMING AND THE AESTHETICS OF IDLENESS

In this book I have largely discussed digital media at the level of general design rather than in terms of the specifics of programming or hardware. I think that it is worthwhile to dip into some of the more technical components of these now, since they have a direct impact on what an event means in programming. Those programming constraints, in turn, will have a subtle influence on the design of UI time.

I would like to focus specifically on the way that programming languages define a user interface event. Such events can include anything that a user might cause to happen: a key stroke, clicking the mouse button (or releasing the button once depressed), pushing on a touch screen device, arriving at a particular GPS location while carrying a mobile device, and so on. As this list suggests, the number of possible events that can be handled by computing

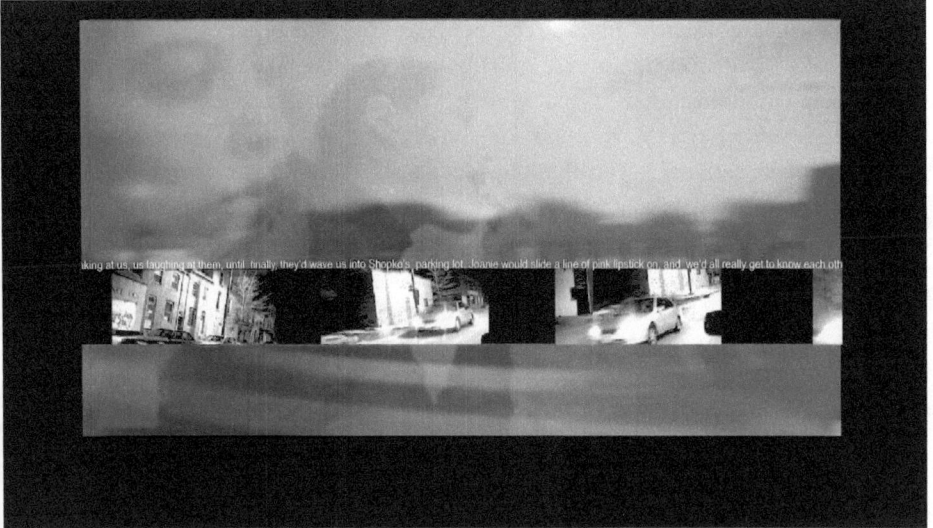

FIGURE 3.2. Ingrid Ankerson and Megan Sapnar, *Cruising*

devices has expanded dramatically in the age of modern and especially mobile computing, as we have moved from keyboard to mouse to touch screen. The evolution of computing from the command line to the GUI (Graphical User Interface) has likewise made event-processing more complex. Instead of simply presenting the user with a flashing cursor and attending to which keys are pressed, the modern computer must also update the mouse pointer position, watch for space on the screen that might trigger some action (menus that drop down when an area is touched by the mouse pointer), and so on. Such computing events are a clear point of interaction between the physical computing device, the platform-specific APIs (Application Programming Interface) that make events recognizable, and the programming language that will do something when that event is recognized.

A key element of the user interface event is that the program specifically has to be watching for it. Attach an unsupported device (perhaps a joystick for games, or a tablet for drawing) to an older computer and no event can be triggered unless device drivers are in place and whatever program is running in the foreground has a method for using that input. In other words, computing devices must be actively watching for an event. For example, the programming language Java makes sense of events using the EventListener class. (A class is a kind of building-block programming template that can be used to create specific functions and data structures.) This class in turn can be implemented in subclasses like MouseListener (which can report things like button clicks) or MouseMotionListener (which signals when the mouse is moved). As the name "listener" in these classes makes clear, any program that is going to take input from the mouse must be actively "listening" for signals from it and will need to have specific instructions that make that event meaningful. In some ways, this is a mundane observation about computers: they can only make sense of events that they have a structure to process, even if that structure involves flashing on the screen a message like "File not found": we might speculate that the only way to "surprise" a computer or application is to cause it to glitch.[5] Unlike all of the other events, such genuine crashes are not anticipated by the software, and thus obviously interrupt the computer's functioning. These events are not part of the program—and therefore not an event in my sense—although they could be part of the user's experience of interacting with that work.

Obviously, the nature of the computing event is not exactly the same thing as the event we theorize in narrative. There is, indeed, a literal similarity to Ryan's definition of the event as a matter of the world state changing based on causality that allows for interpretation. But we can also recognize that such interface events are part of every computing application regardless of how little narrative content this might involve: from a game of Tetris to your interaction with an ATM machine. The fact that a computer can respond to these kinds of user or environmental "events" cannot help us to decide if a particular work has narrativity. But, of course, this structure of digital event is very much *relevant* to those occasions when a digital device is used to create a story. Events in a programming environment must be something that the device is watching for; consequently computers spend their time waiting. Obviously, there is no reason that the artists using these tools to tell stories have to build those stories around waiting, but I would like to argue that such a principle of waiting and device idleness has had a subtle influence on many forms of digital narratives. We have already seen this to be central to *afternoon, House Fire,* and *Cruising,* where the dynamic relationship between contemplative pauses and movement forward is a central design principle. Indeed, we can read *Cruising* in particular as a contemplation about the need to achieve a kind of stasis that makes the story and its reflections on small-town life possible.

---

5. See Peter Krapp's "ludology for losers" (75) focused on the glitch as a component of the video game in *Noise Channels: Glitch and Error in Digital Culture*. In particular, Krapp discusses the aesthetic and rhetorical uses of such disruptions of the expected functioning of the computer.

I would suggest that the common idleness of digital narrative is an aesthetic design influenced but not inevitably caused by the inherent material conditions of the medium—its combination of hardware input methods and programming event structure. Although it is possible to create digital texts in which the time of the story races by, the computing medium nudges designers towards building in such periods of idleness. To show what I mean by the subtle way that idleness can influence digital narrative, and how it might affect our sense of its aesthetics, consider Emily Short's interactive epistolary novel, *First Draft of the Revolution* (2012). Short's digital take on the epistolary novel is especially interesting in its handling of temporality, since the epistolary novel has always struggled with time. Although initially the premise of collecting letters sent back and forth between characters seems to solve narrative problems by providing a simple and realistic motivation for narration, most epistolary novels eventually encounter the problem of narrating rising action. If the author wants to convince the reader that the character is in genuine danger, why is that character writing about the events rather than acting on them? And if the conflict has all been resolved and the suspenseful events are all in the past at the time of writing, it can be difficult to retain a sense of their urgency.

First Draft makes several interesting choices in design that reflect the unique temporality of digital narrative. The basic premise of the story is that the user influences the writing of the letters back and forth between the controlling husband Henri who resides in Paris, and his wife Juliet who has been sent away to the country. The user has a good deal of control over the content of these letters—not so much in terms of the events that are mentioned but rather in how these events are written about. The user can choose to handle topics bluntly or indirectly, to appeal sympathetically to the interlocutor or to threaten or cajole more aggressively. Not all of these choices affect the outcome of the correspondence; as Short explains, the reader's choices are partially aesthetic: "This pattern of choice-making is more contemplative and gentle-paced than one that stakes everything on single decisions. It also, I believe, engages the reader's faculties in a more creative way, because the decisions she's making are partly aesthetic. Does the letter read better this way or that way?"

Short makes one significant choice that affects the temporality of the story: she imagines a magical world in which communication is instantaneous: Juliette "plans her letters on ordinary pages, but when they are ready, she copies them on paper whose enchanted double is hundreds of miles off. The words form themselves on the matching sheaf in her husband's study. No time is wasted on couriers." In some ways the decision seems a bit surprising; this mysterious writing is the only concrete manifestation of magic in the work, and it might initially seem unnecessary. Surely the game can simply handle the time of correspondence the way that print novels do: by leaving these missing weeks of travel time out of the story. To do so, however, would be to change the time dynamic; indeed, we are used to making a choice (triggering an event) in digital narratives and then seeing the result of that action. In other words, we are used to the game waiting for us—rather than the user waiting for the game—either literally or in terms of the represented time of the gameworld.

The choice of writing in this game is also especially significant because it takes as its model a form of everyday activity that has a similar temporal structure: the word processor, like the typewriter and the pad and pen, waits for you to act. In this regard, *First Draft of the Revolution* embodies the fundamental, early temporal logic of the text adventure game, where players progress by typing, and where game time stops and waits for the player to make the next move. Thus, if we recognize waiting as central to digital narrative, then we should expect it to tell different kinds of stories: those less about disruptive events that change the world, and instead about those that embody reflective actions. Indeed, I think that it is no wonder that the first commercially successful game that presented itself primarily as a story, the CD-ROM game *Myst,* was essentially contemplative and built around reading—both the diaries of the characters and the magical books that allowed the player to travel to other spaces. There is nothing inherent in the digital medium that requires time to be handled in this way—just the subtle influence of the structure of the computer event.

Of course there are exceptions to this emphasis on idleness. One of the things that makes the film-like digital works of Young-Hae Chang Heavy Industries so remarkable is that they break with the tradition of user interaction in the digital medium and take complete control of the time of reading. As Warren Liu notes, "In terms of form, their work adamantly refuses to be framed within contemporary posthumanist-inflected evaluations of electronic literature, forsaking the two key elements that function, for many critics, as the foundational characteristics of digital literary texts: interactivity and programmability" (10). These works have caught the attention of critics in part because their sense of time is so different from what we have come to expect of other digital texts. And, of course, such ongoing time is inherent to improvised, real-time digital events—such as those conducted through Twitter or using mobile location services. Rob Wittig and Mark Marino call one of these forms "netprov": "A typical netprov, if such can be described, involves a networked of [sic] platform (such as Twitter, a blog, or Facebook), a set of collaborators, a narrative premise, and a set of constraints. For the most part, netprovs have time limits, although that is not a necessary requirement. Fundamental to netprov is creative play on contemporary platforms" ("Occupy").[6] Likewise, embodied forms of human interaction with computing devices based on physical motion and gesture are much more likely to introduce a stronger sense of continuously progressing time.[7] A well-known example of this kind of embodied interaction is Romy Achituv and Camille Utterback's *Text Rain*, in which participants change the motion of falling letters on a screen based on their own physical location and actions. Such works, though, tend not to be narrative but instead to evoke poetic or conceptual forms of interaction with the work, making the event itself less central. All of these works are exceptions to the temporal dynamics of idleness that I have described, and part of what makes them so striking is that they depart from the more common emphasis on waiting. In general, the tendency to link story and idleness is common in digital narrative, and subtly influenced by the hardware and programming structures through which it is built.

EVENT GRANULARITY

Dynamic of idleness, the detection of an event for which the device is "listening," and some resulting machine action is, then, built into the physical design of computers and the way they are programmed. One implication of this dynamic is greater attention to what I am going to call event "granularity"—the scale of the event triggered by user action, which has implications for our understanding of events in other media.

Recent work on narrative that draws on cognitive theory has provided a framework for discussing narrative events that is particularly important to digital narrative. In *Story Logic*, David Herman summarizes recent work on narrative scripts. Earlier structuralist work on "action sequences" discussed common or "stereotypical" sequences such as a rescue or an abduction (96). The concept of a script generalizes these sequences to apply to our cognitive processing of real-world actions: "I know what to do when the waiter comes up to me in a restaurant because I have been in restaurants before and remember the standard roles of waiter and customer in that setting. Every trip to a restaurant would be an adventure, and would consume far too many cogni-

---

6. See also the explanation on the Meanwhile Netprov site (*http://meanwhilenetprov.com/index.php/what-is-netprov/*) as well as "Netprov: Elements of an Emerging Form."

7. See Rita Raley's discussion of the balance between script and improvisation in locative narratives in "Walk This Way."

tive resources, if I never mastered the appropriate restaurant scripts" (97). These scripts allow readers to make sense of stories even where few details are provided, because we can fill in blanks based on expected features of the event (98).

In this context, it is easy to see how different kinds of narratives would be more or less explicit in how they evoke and fill in details of scripts. A fairy tale or fable might provide only the most basic information necessary to evoke the script (Little Red Riding Hood was walking through the forest on her way to her grandmother's house), while a realist novel may provide copious details about the components of that trip. This kind of granularity to narrative events is something that is particularly important in digital narrative, since there is a complex relationship between the actions of the player (with a mouse pointer, typing in commands, or using a game controller) and the events that occur on-screen. In *Cybertext,* Aarseth notes the gap between player commands and the resulting action in text adventures. While the command "drink scotch" initially evokes a fairly straightforward description of the effect ("You take a small swig of the golden fluid, which burns as it goes down"), when repeated it removes agency from the player and offers a lecture instead: "It's one thing to take a bracer on occasion, but you must resist the temptation to indulge too often" (121). Likewise, Paul Wake has recently noted "the absurd contradiction inherent in the act of witnessing one's own death" in some Choose Your Own Adventure style books, as when a wrong decision results in reader death; as the narration reads, "you never regain consciousness" (203). In all of these cases, there is a variable gap between the actions of the player and the narrated events that result.

It is easy to forget this gap in more realistic video games, but it is a fundamental part of game design. Push a joystick left and the avatar will walk left, but the details of the motion—the turn of the head, the way that the figure moves and comes to a stop—are beyond the player's control, and part of the movement script. This is particularly the case with animations for less common activities. In some games, the command to jump might involve an elaborate crouch and leap, with a grunt as the avatar hauls itself up onto the surface above. Likewise, the common command to reload a weapon in a shooter usually involves an elaborate script that takes several seconds to play through. The time of this action is, of course, why the decision of when to reload is strategic in a larger fight, but it also represents a point at which a simple player command involves a fairly large-grained on-screen action.

The granularity of these events is significant because digital media is a multi-agent environment. I have already touched on this in chapter 1 when

I argued for the broad adoption of the role of intrigue in the design of digital narratives. The virtual presence of the intrigant implies another agent in the work. But I also mean this more literally: in describing the computer as "waiting" I am arguing that there is an active agent at work. Of course, classes like EventListener build upon this idea of an entity that watches for a certain kind of signal, and then springs into action. In chapter 1 I cited Alexander Galloway's discussion, in *Gaming*, of the negotiation of two different kinds of agents, the operator and the machine. As he explains, these agents can create both diegetic and nondiegetic events—that is, those events that take place in the gameworld, and those that do not. Diegetic events might involve movement, combat, or reloading, while non-diegetic events involve adjusting settings or conveying an error message. This issue of event granularity shows us the importance of Galloway's observation that operator and machine frequently participate in the same events. Operator-initiated, diegetic events— that is, the core actions that we think of when playing a video game—are mediated by a machine interpretation that controls a significant part of their appearance and (of course) effect. Galloway's observation that the machine is acting in tandem with the user helps us to understand why event granularity is so important, as well as why waiting is such a central element to our experience of narrative in these media.

CONCLUSION

The interface is usually invisible or taken to be inevitable and unchanging in other media. Often it only becomes visible when there is some kind of material breakdown in the text or its presentation apparatus. Before the era of digital projection, when we watched a film the time of the UI moved forward consistently and unnoticed—unless the film broke and the audience had to sit and wait for it to be restarted. The temporal movement of reading a book only attracts attention when something impedes it, such as when pages are torn out or scrambled. Of course, many artistic experiments with the form of the book were designed precisely to draw our attention to what we can call the UI of traditional reading, from the somewhat baffling multicolumn printing of Steve Katz's *The Exagggerations of Peter Prince* (1968) to the postcard design of Robert Filliou's *Ample Food for Stupid Thought* (1965). Recent digital versions of the film or book draw our attention to this overlooked interface. Modern computer-based DVD film systems introduce a UI at the top level of the disk menu, allowing viewers to jump to a particular scene, modify the audio, or restart the film from the beginning. Likewise, the time of reading becomes more visible in ebook readers. Amazon's Kindle, for example, estimates the remaining reading time in a chapter based on previous page turns.

As with the narrative concepts discussed in previous chapters, these digital translations encourage us to ask what relevance the concept of UI time might have to pre-digital, nonexperimental texts. In retrospect, we might recognize that print has always been able to impose time on the process of reading through, for example, serial publication.[8] Likewise, the changing landscape of television has resulted in very different distribution models that, in turn, transform the UI time of watching. Many of us consume seasons of a television show by "binge watching" multiple episodes at a time. This has been possible ever since production companies discovered that there was a market for boxed set editions of television seasons. Netflix, in particular, has been experimenting with different kinds of distribution timelines—making the full season of some shows available all at once on their initial release.

I have already argued in the previous chapters that digital narrative draws attention to the issue of use by presenting the story as an artifact with which the reader interacts in various ways. This chapter provides another element of the use of digital artifacts. Here the UI has a time in which the reader operates—from the infinitely patient game to the rushing time of Young-Hae Chang Heavy Industries. On reflection, the same is true of other media—from the immediate accessibility of the modern novel to the required patience of the Victorian serial. In all of these cases, we encounter the UI time of use.

---

8. The Victorian Serial Novels website (*http://victorianserialnovels.org*) makes this particularly clear by organizing the month-by-month publications of various novels. As the site explains, "You can navigate to a particular month and year to read installments of novels that came out simultaneously. We are calling a group of novels whose serial parts overlapped a 'stack.'" Thinking about overlapping novels as stacks implies a very different sense of the temporality of reading them.

CHAPTER 4

Number and Movement in the Construction of Digital Characters

THE IDEA of character in digital narrative is strangely undertheorized. We have already noted extensive work on space and setting, on the idea of narration in games, and on time and progression. But the characters that populate digital narratives can be, it seems, taken for granted. The perennial urge to turn video games into films (and vice versa) so often is based on the feeling that characters will carry across different media. Luke Skywalker is supposed to be the same character, whether he is in a movie or a video game.[1] This may explain why character in digital media has seemed to be a topic that requires less theory or analysis.

In this chapter I will argue that this attitude is wrong, and that digital media gives us a chance to think about some of our most fundamental assumptions about the nature of character itself. To provide a framework for re-evaluating digital characters, I will depend on John Frow's 2014 *Character and Person*. Frow's wide-ranging study is, likewise, an attempt to question some of our most basic ideas about character—in particular, the seemingly

---

1. Within narrative theory we can see this particularly clearly in the way that possible world theories so often use fictional characters as exactly what moves between the real and fictional world, or between one and another possible world. Thomas Pavel opens *Fictional Worlds* (1986) by taking the example of how we discuss Samuel Pickwick. We might go back to Saul Kripke's *Naming and Necessity* (1972) for a discussion of identity across possible worlds (42). In all of these cases, the individual figure (historical or fictional character) is taken to be the simplest entity that can move between history, text, and medium.

natural association of characters and persons. In this chapter I am particularly interested in two points of entry into Frow's book. First, his interest in the way that character performs a compositional, pragmatic role in the narrative works against the idea that characters are important because of their continuities with real-world people. This compositional facet of character is, we will see, particularly relevant to digital characters, who are often used by the player to *do* things—navigate the world, progress the narration, change the view we have on a particular scene. Second, Frow notes that characters are related to types, and that one of the central dynamics in literary character is what he calls "scale." I will show that digital narrative depends heavily on a certain kind of multiplicity, and that Frow's reflections on scale have a particular manifestation in many forms of digital storytelling.

POINT OF ACTION AND THE CHARACTER AS FIGURE

What makes some on-screen representations of the user seem like characters and others not? It is easy to think of a 3D person-shaped representation controlled by the user while playing the game as a *character*, but why not treat our mouse pointer as a character acting on the space of a virtual desktop? Recent work on digital narrative has made us aware of the importance of a distinction first introduced by Britta Neitzel between the "point of view" from which the action is seen, and the "point of action" on which the player may act within the game space. Drawing on Genette's distinction between "who speaks" and "who sees"—that is between the narrator and the focalizer—Neitzel proposes a parallel structure for Point of Action (PoA, in contrast to PoV) which likewise can be located within or without the gameworld. Recent books by Jan-Noël Thon and Dave Ciccoricco build upon Neitzel's work. Ciccoricco links this idea of a point of action to Thierry Bardini's observations about the mouse pointer as a similar point of action: "Indeed, the mouse pointer is in effect a literal, analog representation or translation of the reader's movement in the text" (Ciccoricco 75, citing Bardini, "Bridging"). Ciccoricco's extension of Neitzel and Bardini is helpful in drawing our attention to the fact that user participation in digital spaces does not always depend on a realistic avatar, and making clear that there is continuity between our experience of steering a character through game space and manipulating files on a virtual desktop. Rune Klevjer warns against collapsing this distinction entirely: "We must make a distinction between 'avatar' understood as a playable character (or persona) and 'avatar' understood as a vehicle through which the player is given some kind of embodied agency and presence within the gameworld" (17). It is tempting to adopt the "cursor analogy" and see the avatar as the latter, but he argues that our phenomenological experience is more complex:

> At the heart of the player-avatar relationship lies a tension and a paradox, reflected in our intuitive understanding of what it means to be immersed in a navigable 3D environment through an avatar. How can we say that the player is extending or reaching into the gameworld, while at the same time also saying that the player is 'being within' and 'acting from within' the gameworld? How can the avatarial embodiment be both a kind of extension and a kind of re-location at the same time? (Klevjer 20)

Klevjer argues convincingly that this paradox is unique to digital environments.

The player/avatar relationship is the only element of digital characters that has been the subject of extensive scholarly work. Nietzel provides an important context for this relationship: how we act on a gameworld is a unique element of digital textuality, and this point of action need not be a representation of a human person—even though that is commonly the case. Indeed, scholarship on the way that players interact with the gameworld through an avatar has depended heavily on anthropomorphic identification. Sherry Turkle's 1995 *Life on the Screen: Identity in the Age of the Internet* painted a sympathetic image of how players could explore identities and build communities in an online, "virtual" environment. In retrospect, this early work was a bit naive in suggesting that an online environment "provides ample room for individuals to express unexplored parts of themselves" (185). More recent work has delved into how players construct identities in such environments, recognizing that a significant part of these identities will vary based not just on the mechanical conditions of the game environment, but also on the cultural and community expectations unique to each world.[2]

Most of the scholarship in this area has contrasted our experience of on-screen digital characters to other media like film, rather than challenging this anthropomorphic identification as the basis for our experience of these elements. In the influential collection *First Person*, Ken Perlin makes a simple observation about the difference between novel and game that I cited in passing in chapter 1. I would like to quote him at greater length here:

---

2. On the way that game mechanics influence this relationship, see Sonia Fizek and Monika Wasilewska's "Embodiment and Gender Identity in Virtual Worlds." On community, see *Digital Culture, Play, and Identity,* and Cecelia Pearce and Artemesia's discussion of "The *Uru* diaspora" in *Communities of Play.*

> So, there is something very particular about the way the novel, in all its many variants, goes about its business. By telling us a story, it asks us to set aside our right to make choices—our agency. Instead, the agency of a protagonist takes over, and we are swept up in observation of his struggle, more or less from his point of view, as though we were some invisible spirit or angel perched upon his shoulder, watching but never interfering.
>
> By way of contrast, look at games. A game does not force us to relinquish our agency. In fact, the game depends on it.
>
> When you play *Tomb Raider* you don't actually think of Lara Croft as a person the same way, say, you think of Harry Potter as a person [. . .]. There is a fictional construct in the backstory to the game. But while you're playing the game, the very effectiveness of the experience depends on *you* becoming Lara Croft. The humanlike figure you see on your computer screen is really a game token, and every choice she makes, whether to shoot, to leap, to run, to change weapons, is your choice. (13–14)

Perlin is correct, I think, that the player's identification with an on-screen representation is more complex precisely because the character seems to be performing contradictory roles—both as a point of player action and as an object of narrative that we are watching unfold. In a relatively early essay on this topic also focused on the Lara Croft character, Mary Flanagan theorized that the on-screen avatar has five different points on the action/identification scale: 1) players use the character to act; 2) the avatar acts independently through minor "idle animations" such as breathing or swaying; 3) the player adventures "with" the avatar as a kind of on-screen companion; 4) players may watch the character as an object of spectatorship; and 5) the player may identify with the avatar.[3] Although we might quibble with the details of Flanagan's account, I think that she correctly describes the range of player/avatar relationships that, as this list implies, can contain contradictions.[4]

---

3. In *Gaming at the Edge*, Adrienne Shaw analyzes the advertising language for the Lara Croft games, which refers both to "accompanying" the avatar as the player, and "stepping into the role" of the heroine (60). She develops this as a distinction between identification *as* and *with* game characters (78). Ragnhild Tronstad's "Character Identification in *World of Warcraft*" discusses James Newman's claim that character capacity, rather than appearance, is usually more important in engagement and immersion. See Newman, "The Myth of the Ergodic Video Game."

4. We should be cautious not to focus on the technical qualities of the digital medium at the expense of the social. Writing about role-playing games, Esther MacMallum-Stewart and Justin Parsler note that consciously role-playing involves "seeking to create a character who transcends the mechanic of the game and takes on a plausible, defined reality of its own" (226).

This work on the player/avatar relationship is valuable in its way, but I think that it misses some of the more radical ways that digital narrative can challenge our assumptions about characters. It is on this point that John Frow's *Character and Person* is so valuable in asking fundamental questions with the goal of "framing a positive understanding of this ontologically ambivalent construct which lies at the heart of the life of textual fictions of all kinds." He goes on to explain the need to resist simply applying our models from everyday life:

> How can we understand fictional character both as a formal construct, made out of words or images and having a fully textual existence, and as a set of effects which are modelled on the form of the human person? The danger of thinking of it in terms of this modelling is that we commit the category error of abstracting character from its textual existence and treating it as though it had an independent presence. (vi)

It is not that the player/avatar relation is irrelevant—in fact, Frow has a discussion of this himself in this book—but that these avatars reinforce our natural tendency to think of on-screen entities as persons with an independent presence.[5] In fact, the transmedial nature of so many entertainment franchises depends, in part, on seeing these ludic on-screen entities as "people" who can appear in multiple games, as well as in films and novels.

In this chapter I want to emphasize the "textual existence" of these on screen figures. Bardini's example of the mouse pointer as a possible avatar is a worthwhile counterexample to this assumption of personhood. In many ways, Lara Croft is just as much a "point of action" as the mouse pointer. Frow addresses this textuality directly at the outset of his chapter on character as a "figure" when he asks "whether and to what extent character must be seen as unified and coherent ('handsome, clever, and rich'), and, indeed, whether and to what extent it must look like a person at all" (2). Specifically, I would like to consider what these on-screen characters *do* in digital narratives as the corollary to what Frow describes as the textual existence of characters in print and other media.

---

5. Frow describes our relation to the avatar as "layered." Noting that our engagement with games is frequently "kinaesthetic" and grounded in movement and action more than identification with the avatar, he concludes that "rather than positing a single point of identification (the avatar, kinaesthetic immersion, the logic of computation), we should perhaps posit instead a hierarchy of levels of identification, the 'layered positionings'" he proposed earlier in the book (48).

Broadly, Frow frames his discussion as an examination of two schools within scholarship on character: the structuralist reduction of character to a formal typology of roles, and the humanist assumption of "plentitude," in which character exceeds its role in the story and instead can be treated as a full person (17).[6] While the structuralist sees character merely as "a paradigm constructed cumulatively across the length of a text as successive sets of semantic differentiation" (12), the humanist approach lends itself to ethical analysis, which is "at its simplest [. . .] the discussion of the moral make-up (the *ēthos*) of characters, as though they were acquaintances whose virtues and shortcomings one were discussing" (15–16). He summarizes his approach to understanding the "figurative" nature of character as follows:

> Fictional character is a person-shaped figure made salient by a narrative ground. As figure, it is a dimension of the compositional structure of a text, a moment of an action sequence which both drives and acquires attributes from the sequence. Through that process of attribution of qualities character takes the form of a semantic culture, accumulating (progressively or discontinuously, coherently or incoherently) through the course of a text. But character is, in certain respects, also the analogue of "real" persons, conforming more or less closely and more or less fully to the schemata that govern, in any particular society, what it means to be a person and to have a physical body, a moral character, a sense of self, and a capacity for action. I say "in certain respects" because fictional character happens in accordance with the modes of being specified by particular genres; it is of the order of representation rather than of the order of the real. (24–5)

There is a lot to unpack in this passage, but what is most important from my perspective is the balance that Frow is trying to strike between personness and its textuality. His insight that our ability to import our expectations about real-world persons depends on genre strikes me as important, and one that has implications for digital textuality. Equally important is the emphasis on the compositional role that character plays in the text. It is that emphasis on the narrative and ludic *function* of the on-screen character that has been missing in so much work on the player/avatar relationship. Frow's analysis in

---

6. This is not to suggest that Frow is the first person to situate character theory through a tension between structuralism and theories that are more humanist in orientation. Thomas Pavel opens his 1986 *Fictional Worlds* with a critique of structuralism to set up his own "referential theory of fiction" (9). In his 1989 *Reading People, Reading Plots*, James Phelan offers his rhetorical theory of narrative as organizing thematic, mimetic, and synthetic qualities of characters. And more recently Alex Woloch's *The One vs. The Many* describes the "character space" as "between person and form."

Character and Person invites us to ask a more far-reaching question: what do digital characters *do* for their texts? As we consider this question, we should also keep in mind Frow's suspicion towards the overapplication of our ideas about persons from the real world. In other words, I would like to be particularly attentive to the ways that the digital character's function takes us away from our conventional (humanistic) ideas about character as an entity whose interest is primarily a matter of moral analysis and understanding.

One of the most media-specific roles for character in digital narrative is as a vehicle for managing our point of view on the scene. Indeed, while we often have to introduce students to different kinds of narration in our literature classes, the distinction between first-person and third-person game perspectives is part of the lingua franca of video game fandom. The ubiquity of this point of view language depends on the way that the camera metaphor has been imported to digital media from film.[7] At the beginning of *The Language of New Media*, Lev Manovich argues that "cinematic ways of seeing the world, of structuring time, of narrating a story, of linking one experience to the next, have become the basic means by which computer users access and interact with all cultural data" (xv). His focus is primarily on editing and montage (xviii), but I would suggest that there is a broader and more pervasive assumption of visuality and the camera metaphor that finds its way from film into computing. The language of the virtual camera has particularly depended on a broader assumption about the fundamentally spatial nature of digital worlds and objects. In 1979 F. K. Stanzel made "mediacy" central to his theory of narrative, but also noted that the specific spatiality of narration—so central to filmic mise-en-scène—was not a part of the Victorian novel. He contrasts the perspectival narrators of Joyce and Woolf to the aperspectival writing of Dickens and Thackeray. He explains: "Every perception, every expression of a narrator's thought originates from a standpoint which not only can be defined more or less accurately according to its spatial and temporal distance from the action, but also according to the degree of its insight into the external and internal events" (20). Stanzel nicely separates out the literal and metaphorical meaning of "point of view," recognizing that the more literal positioning of a viewer is part of a larger sense of how we use the term.

The link between film and this more spatial understanding of narrative is captured at the end of Scholes and Kellogg's 1966 *The Nature of Narrative*. In the final few pages of their chapter on point of view, Scholes and Kellogg

---

7. In contrast, in the earlier essay "Playing at Being: Psychoanalysis and the Avatar" (2003), Bob Rehak takes a Lacanian approach, seeing the experience as primarily one of spectatorship (103).

shift their attention "in the direction of the future" (279) by noting that film promises to reshape point of view:

> To understand how the camera-projector point of view distinguishes film from stage drama, the reader need only remind himself of the difference between attending a football or baseball game in person and watching one on television. In the stadium the spectator responds to the total scene unfolding before him. His eye looks where it will, at whatever aspect of the scene catches its notice. But the televised game is seen through the camera eye, with its long shots and close-ups, the vocal commentary of the announcer, the time dislocation of the video-tape replay with its shifts in point of view. Sport is not art, of course, but we apprehend it either as drama or narrative depending on whether we observe it directly or perceive it through a medium which filters it through a point of view. (280)

Scholes and Kellogg see film as embodying and literalizing the issue of point of view by insisting on a spatial and temporal location for every shot.

In his more recent work, Manovich has shown that this kind of spatial thinking and virtual camera is built into the software used to create and edit three-dimensional digital objects. The emergence of three-dimensional editing has co-opted film, subordinating film's lens-based composition to a larger computer-manipulated three-dimensional world, as Manovich argues:

> A designer positions all the elements which go into a composition—2D animated sequences, 3D objects, particle systems, video and digitized film sequences, still images and photographs—inside the shared 3D virtual space. There these elements can be further animated, transformed, blurred, filtered, etc. So while all moving image media has been reduced to the status of hand-drawn animation in terms of their manipulability, we can also state that all media have become layers in 3D space. In short, the new media of 3D computer animation has "eaten up" the dominant media of the industrial age—lens-based photo, film, and video recording. (*Software* 294)

In this passage, Manovich is arguing that new software structures transform and reconfigure older media. I want to emphasize, however, how much this 3D modeling depends on cinematic assumptions about how to represent space and event. This is especially the case in recent commercial video games, where the dominant assumption is that they will obey a three-dimensional logic of camera positioning.

The overwhelming popularity of this 3D authoring of games is particularly ironic because the limitations of this understanding of digital representation are immediately obvious. Digital tools provide a way of visualizing data that need not be tethered to a traditional "point of view" on real-world three-dimensional objects. And, of course, early digital games richly explored the possibilities of representation before three-dimensional video became possible and, then, dominant. This is true not only of side-scrolling games that have only two dimensions, but also to text games. These obviously include text adventure games, but also educational games like *The Oregon Trail*, and early resource simulation games like *Hamurabi*. Nonetheless, digital media has broadly adopted this spatial model for its worlds and objects, and this has implications for what Frow would call the "compositional" role of characters in these works. Simply put, I will try to show that characters are a vehicle by which the player navigates and explores the world. Characters are tools for seeing, in other words.

CHARACTER AS PUPPET

To get at the way characters in digital media serve the compositional purpose of movement and exploration, let us turn back to Espen Aarseth's *Cybertext*, and its skepticism towards applying traditional narrative terms and categories to digital works. Aarseth cites Mary Jane Sloane's description of the main character in a text adventure game as a "puppet" (113) to describe the physical character that the player steers through the gameworld: "When it comes to perspective, there seems to be an unclear boundary between the voice and the player's puppet" (120), noting that sometimes the game simply describes what the player commands and at others offers elaborate narratives in response to player commands. Aarseth gives the example of the response in *Deadline* to the command "Analyze teacup for ebullion": "Sergeant Duffy walks up as quietly as a mouse. He takes the cup from you. 'I'll return soon with the results,' he says, and leaves as silently as he entered" (119). Puppets are not characters in the traditional sense because their purpose is not to behave realistically or consistently. In the text adventure game, the purpose of the puppet is to allow the player to navigate the gameworld, rather than to be a psychologically interesting character.

This is an insight that applies well to the notion of a camera-based character in the 3D game as well. In *Prince of Persia: The Sands of Time* (2003), each mission begins by flying the camera through the level (in a mimetically unjustified way) in order to give the player a sense of the spatial goal of the mission. Often moving the player (or the camera where that is supported) is necessary in order to understand a challenge or puzzle. Typical is a puzzle in the "Sanctuary" mission in *Uncharted* (2007) in which the player must rotate statues in order to open up a secret door, but can do so only by consulting the compass mosaic on the floor for reference (see figure 4.1). Here part of the task is positioning the avatar so that the spatial reference provided by the compass can be seen. In this sense, the character is a literal point of view, and a sense of interiority is replaced with an all-encompassing visuality. *Uncharted* does a particularly good job of showing how the manipulation of perspective and avatar movement can be an element of puzzle-solving. Other games make movement itself part of the challenge—either by presenting a maze-like space that the player must learn to navigate, or by making the movement difficult, as in the case where the player avatar must make a perfectly timed jump over a chasm. In all of these cases, moving the avatar through space is itself part of what makes gameplay successful.

Of course, there is a literary tradition that these sorts of digital narratives are drawing on as they link movement and character. Progression through most games is marked by literal spatial movement, and it is common in games of all genres for completion of a segment of the game to "unlock" a next area, which most often can then be revisited at will. In common design strategy, progression through the game makes more and more spaces available to the player. This game design depends on the heroic movement forward which is also a development of the character. Perhaps the most straightforward example of this structure is Dante's *Divine Comedy*, which narrates the movement of the hero through Inferno, Purgatory, and eventually Paradise to God. Movement is related to encounter and thus insight, which in turn then enables further movement; character is indexed to place. This is the core of the pilgrimage narrative structure. In his classic work on allegory, Angus Fletcher describes the "progress" model for allegory:

> There is usually a paradoxical suggestion that by leaving home the hero can return to another better "home": Christian leaves the City of Destruction, where his family home is, to reach the true home of all believers, the Celestial City. Sometimes, having made the journey, the hero comes back to his original home so much changed that he cannot any longer hold his former position: of this Gulliver would be a case; in his story there is a suggestion that his voyage has removed any chance he might have of returning to a resting place. Self-knowledge is apparently the goal, and with a disil-

FIGURE 4.1. *Uncharted: Drake's Fortune*

lusioned image of the self before him, Gulliver cannot tolerate his "home" or his family. (151–2)

This is a common, although certainly not universal, model for the quest. Physical movement becomes a way of charting intellectual, physical, or spiritual development.

The counterexample of this strong link between place and identity is the travelogue, which is usually closer to the puppet model that Aarseth describes. The traveling character is merely a tool for the travel—a vehicle, as it were—whose experiences may tell us something about the places visited and the sights seen, but where character is largely incidental to the appeal of the work. I have in mind, in particular, Edward Said's account of European travels in *Orientalism,* where resisting the influence of place and remaining unchanged is a central challenge, and part of the work that the travel account accomplished: "Every European traveler or resident of the Orient has had to protect himself from its unsettling influences. [. . .]. The eccentricities of Oriental life, with its odd calendars, its exotic spatial configurations, its hopelessly strange languages, its seemingly perverse morality, were reduced considerably when they appeared as a series of detailed items presented in a normative European prose style" (166–7). In 1995 Mary Fuller and Henry Jenkins recognized the link between many video games and the travelogue. Focusing specifically on Nintendo, they argued that "the movement in space that the rescue plot seems to motivate is itself the point, the topic, and the goal and that this shift in emphasis from narrativity to geography produces features that make Nintendo and New World narratives in some ways strikingly similar to each other and different from many other kinds of texts" (58). The "locodescriptive form" depends on movement as exploration that is specifically connected to advancement through the game. Taking the specific example of the savepoint, they write, "The games also often create a series of goalposts that not only marks our progress through the game space but also determines our dominance over it. Once you've mastered a particular space, moving past its goalpost, you can reassume play at the point no matter the outcome of a particular round" (67).

A good example of how these models work in practice is the MMORPG *Lord of the Rings Online*. Players create characters not in the original novels, but travel through the familiar landscape and occasionally interact with characters from the books at the same time that the main plot of the novel is unfolding. It is easy to see why this game is particularly exemplary. *The Lord of the Rings* is a classic heroic quest narrative, and the movement of the characters (in particular, Frodo Baggins) from naivety about the larger world through exploration and deepening knowledge of the nature of the ring in the end allows him to complete the quest and destroy it. Movement across the landscape in the novel is one of the means by which Frodo comes to understand the world and the magic that empowers the ring. This is a classic example of a quest in which movement across the landscape is entwined with the transformation of the character necessary to complete the quest.

Lord of the Rings Online embodies this relationship between movement and character by associating world region with character level. As players complete quests and gain levels, new regions become explorable. The player moves from starting regions in the Shire, through Bree and Rivendell, eventually through Gondor towards Mordor. Although some video games lock access to areas explicitly by simply making them inaccessible until some condition is met, *Lord of The Rings Online* gates movement by populating the landscape with different-level creatures, so that a low-level character will be killed quickly by random encounters if that character happens to wander into a higher-level region. It is clear that this movement is part of the motivation for developing higher-level characters: players who are fans of the original book want to get to see Rivendell and Minas Tirith and meet famous characters from the books in those regions, and thus need to develop a character capable of surviving in those spaces. In this regard, this game provides an interesting counterexample to our tendency to discuss digital avatars as a source of player identification. This example makes clear that character development is also a matter of opening up spaces and activities. Although *Lord of the Rings Online* makes this particularly obvious with its geography-based progression, this motivation for character development is true of many other games, where parts of the game (multiplayer combat, raids, character class options) are gated by progression.

THE CHARACTER PUPPET AND ALTMAN'S THEORY OF FOLLOWING

Although the example of *Lord of The Rings Online* suggests some continuities with print, I am suggesting that the link between character and movement is central to most digital works. This link represents what Frow calls a compositional feature of character—a point at which these digital characters obey the necessity of the design and use of the medium, rather than the humanistic models that we might import from our knowledge of real-world people.

Rick Altman's *A Theory of Narrative* links movement and narration, and so provides a valuable way to identify what is distinct about characters in digital narrative. Altman works to shift narrative theory away from an exclusive focus on the novel to narrative in its other forms. In particular, Altman jettisons the issue of point of view, in favor of the much broader notion of "following." "Imagine a long shot of the Grand Central Station waiting room," Altman writes. Initially the camera is unmoving, simply filming the scene.

> When the camera focuses on a single individual and follows her, however, we recognize that we are being cued to read this scene as narrative. Followed, the character serves as a vector defining the space before us. As she becomes a character, thanks to the process of following, so her activities—previously indistinguishable from all the other activities visible in the image—turn into narrative-defining actions. Constitutive of narrative, the process of following thus simultaneously activates both character and narrator. (16)

While "point of view" is "applicable only to selected texts" (22), particularly the modern novel, following is universal to anything that could be considered narrative. As he notes, as soon as the description begins to follow one figure, the character emerges from a sea of other individuals, and the work of the narrator in describing the scene becomes clear. Character and narration emerge at the same moment.

Altman's account of narrative is obviously provocative, and seeks to upset many of the common models of narration and focalization that are fundamental to current theory. It would certainly seem to be the case that Altman's theory of following overlooks the subtlety with which the narration can interact with the mind of the character that moves through the landscape. In particular, a great deal of narrative theory has examined the relationship and tension between the scene as it is seen and the words used to describe it. By associating the narrator with a camera following an individual, Altman seems to elide this distinction. Altman's theory is designed to address some of these problems by disengaging from the details of narrator or focalizer, and by examining the rhythms of whom the text is following more generally. Altman offers the concept of the "following-unit" such that the text is "a series of segments made up of that portion of the text where a character (or group of characters) is followed continuously" (22). But it is clear that, in focusing on the higher-level issue of the construction of the text and the movement between characters, Altman's theory is less attentive to the way that the text can communicate character thoughts and attitudes than is addressed by focalization. Even if we overlook the issue of focalization to embrace Altman's theory of following, work on description in writing suggests that even static scenes involve the active movement of authorial attention across the scene. Jeffrey Kittay writes about the movement of the eye in description: "The percipient can also trace with his eye a *parcour,* one that a surface itself may suggest, as it often has lines of possible relationships and, of course, a frame. We must note however that this 'trip' is a closed one, ultimately reaffirming the frame as closure, the surface as limit. It is a trip that has an 'about-ness' to it, the de- of *description*"[8] (229). As Kittay suggests, in writing the process of description itself is an action that requires movement. Indeed, Altman's filmic example is in many ways an outlier among other media and how movement allows the process of narration to emerge.[9]

---

8. As with other chapters, any emphasis in quotes is from the original text, unless otherwise noted.

9. See also Chatman's discussion of description in film. He notes that "there seems no *need* for films to describe; it is their nature to show—and show continuously—a cornucopia of visual details" (39) before going on to show how film can, indeed, describe in part by movement (45) in terms that resonate with Altman's theory.

Despite all of these limitations, Altman's theory is valuable for our account of video games because it provides a framework for characterizing the relationship between movement and our sense of narration. In fact, it is precisely the way that digital narrative challenges Altman's account of narration that helps us to see this unique compositional element of digital characters. Obviously, many games directly depend on Altman's "following-unit" modulations. For example, the recent *Assassin's Creed Syndicate* (2015) takes turns following the twins Jacob and Evie Frye, whom the player controls for different missions. Here, the player is quite literally following one character and then the other in very much the same way that a novel might do so between one chapter and the next. More important, however, is the fact that our sense of moving *through* the world with the character is central to our experience of these games. Although Altman offers his theory as applying to narrative more generally, I think I have shown that the experience of steering the player avatar is particularly important to digital narrative, where it has some distinctive features. In the traditional narratives that Altman describes, the emergence of character and the role of narrating the character's movements are two sides of the same coin: they become evident at the exact same moment. As soon as we recognize that the attention of the camera (or narrator) is focused on a particular individual, we think of that individual as a character and the rest as background setting. In the case of digital narrative in which the player is steering the avatar through the landscape, agency is subtly different. The game designer has linked movement to a particular individual in the landscape (thus picking out one person from a potential crowd), but it is the player who subsequently reveals the landscape through gameplay. In other words, in digital narrative the tight connection between movement and the agency of the narration that Altman theorizes is broken.

Jan-Noël Thon discusses a particularly extreme instance of the way that the player appears to be involved in the unfolding narration of a game. He notes that player action triggers prerecorded bits of voice-over narration in the game *Prince of Persia*. In this game the player-controlled title character appears to be narrating the gameplay events as they unfold from the perspective of a future self:

> The player of *Price of Persia: Sands of Time* interacts with the game spaces according to specific game rules, and some of the resulting ludic events "trigger" certain prerecorded "pieces" of verbal narration—in other words, the gameplay causes the narratorial representation. [. . .] The gameplay as well as the regularly appearing cut-scenes are clearly marked as contribut-

ing to the representation of the latter's "barely hypodiegetic" secondary storyworld, which allows the player to pretend that the gameplay has already happened—at least as far as it can be comprehended as contributing to the representation of the storyworld that the verbal narration attributable to the Prince's narrating evokes. (215)

The player controls an on-screen character who is narrating the on-screen events from a hypothetical point of view after the events have occurred. Perhaps the best-known (and cleverest) manifestation of this odd temporality is what the narration says when the player fails and causes the on-screen character to die: "No no no, that's not how it happened." This retrospective narration caused by player action is, as he notes, "mildly paradoxical," but the tension between the agency of the player and the on-screen events is inherent in any game. I am not arguing, of course, that the centrality of following in these games means that the player is somehow "coauthoring" the work, or that the player *is* the narrator. I am suggesting, instead, that the connection between movement and the emergence of the story out of the narrator/character relationship is changed in these sorts of video games, where the player has a role in revealing the landscape in a way that is not accounted for well by Altman's simpler filmic example.

It is precisely because our use of characters to explore the world in digital narrative does not line up well with film that Altman's theory helps to reveal the particular compositional demands of this medium. The revelation of the landscape via character movement is based not on the intention of a narrator, but rather on the actions of the player. And yet, it is clear that the landscape images that we see are not *created* in any way by the player, even if his or her actions are the ones that trigger their display. This world is designed to be seen but the actions that cause particular parts of the world to be revealed are those of the player. We need a way to talk about the landscape as a designed feature upon which the player must act. This might remind us of the concept of intrigue discussed in chapter 1. There I argued that intrigue was an often-adversarial system against which the player must act to progress the game. Here, likewise, the landscape has what we might call a variable degree of "friction" that often resists the players' desire to reveal new spaces, and steers movement in certain ways.

In trying to describe the friction of the landscape, I think that it is helpful to return to Altman, and to consider another part of his theory, the importance that he assigns to framing. Altman distinguishes between narrative as a quality and narrative as a thing—*some* narrative vs. *a* narrative (17)—which will remind us of Ryan's distinction between narrative and narrativity. For him, events become a narrative by being framed: "Daytime television soap operas offer a good example of 'some' narrative. No matter when we tune in, we are rapidly convinced that we are dealing with a narrative text; yet no matter how long we watch, we never reach closure. Unlike most novels and films, soaps are all middle" (17–18). For Altman, events become a narrative when they are "framed" in a way that provides a beginning, middle, and end—thus making clear "a common narrative pattern" (18) that lets us identify the narrative with a particular plot type. When we encounter a work that is all middle—and thus has "some" narrative without being framed in a way that makes it "a" narrative—we lack a sense of the overall trajectory of the work, its plot pattern.

Altman's observation about the importance of recognizing a pattern that provides a sense of narrative arc is helpful in teasing apart what else we need besides following to have "a" narrative. As he explains, "Just as a shot of the crowds in Grand Central Station becomes narrative (in the sense of 'some' narrative) only when a character is followed, thus revealing narrational activity, so a series of events becomes narrative (in the sense of 'a' narrative) only when those events are framed" (18). I actually think the example of the soap opera is a misleading one, since such stories work precisely because they are framed by conventional narrative plots that allow us to anticipate the likely beginnings and endings even if we have seen only occasional episodes. But his theory encourages us to think about the way that digital narrative can impose a frame on seemingly incomplete activities. Indeed, we might see this as a particular challenge in video games, where designers cannot anticipate the time of play or the order of events, and thus must find other ways of creating a feeling of narrative. For this reason, the mechanical structuring of movement in a digital narrative is particularly relevant. The example of gating that I have discussed above represents a partial solution. An MMORPG like *Lord of the Rings Online* is profoundly invested in the middle of the story. The fact that the world exists in a suspended state, and that players may well spend months or even years without the world (and its implied story) appearing to move forward means that it pushes the in media res logic beyond the soap opera. And yet, precisely by inserting a gating mechanism into the world, a game like this can provide a narrative arc, and thus a frame. We know where the game is going in part because we know the books on which it is based, but also because we can look at the world map and chart the movement of the game forward. The framing of the narrative can be created through the organization of space and possible movement, and that organization is the designed element upon which the player acts by moving the character.

Although *Lord of the Rings Online* is in some ways a quirky example—based on a book and tied so closely to geography as it is—it raises the issue of how game mechanics can function to frame player actions. As we saw in chapter 2, other games rely heavily on the orienting space to provide a sense of the overall arc of the game. All game space is designed to distinguish between the trivial and the significant. For the *Lord of the Rings Online,* this is the progression from the Shire to Mordor; for a first-person shooter, it is the distinction between pressing forward into a space with enemies and remaining in a safe starting area or place where enemies have already been defeated. Altman's account helps us to see how these rules create a context for the player actions that complicate the character/narrator relationship in other media. As we have seen, in film, character and narration emerge at the same moment of movement; in digital narrative, the central character's movement depends on mechanical rules built into the game. The space waits to be explored, but we know that the conditions for our exploration are constrained in very specific ways. Consider the difference between the experience of navigating a game space like *Lord of the Rings Online* and a space unstructured by gameplay like Google Maps. Of course, it is possible for narrative to emerge out of the use of Google Maps—anyone who has told a harrowing story about being directed incorrectly by driving directions has done so. But the way that space is structured by a game makes movement meaningful in and of itself—did you complete a particular level, discover a hidden area?—independent of the uses to which this space is put by pragmatic goals. Because movement is structured by the design of the environment, we can see a creative agency at work. Moving around Middle Earth feels "framed" in a way that using Google Maps does not precisely because we understand that the former is built for a narrative purpose that makes some locations and movements meaningful and possible, and others unimportant or impossible.[10]

This gameplay space is obviously designed to challenge the player and shape what we are able to see on screen based on movement and camera angles, as well as the way that some actions can result in voice-over narration and cut-

---

10. We should be careful not to overlook the subtle way in which frames can be introduced into even seemingly innocuous mappings. Carpenter's *In Absentia*, which I discussed in chapter 2, raises a broader question about the way that any form of mapping imposes a kind of frame on space. Carpenter's decision to introduce personal, disordered anecdotes into a landscape mapped by Google is a way of challenging corporate utility and private ownership of space. Google provides a sort of framing for city space that is not narrative, but is definitely predisposed to certain kinds of uses. Part of the brilliance of *In Absentia* is teasing out those predispositions, and looking for other ways to organize this space and tell stories.

scenes. Because those constraints and mechanical conditions for movement and action are different from any sort of voice that might provide narration, they are part of a broader system of intrigue. In chapter 1 we have seen that intrigue can be used to describe all of those mechanical parts of the work as an artifact with which the reader or player must interact, independently of the voice or voices that are providing narration. Applied to the mechanics of avatar movement, we can say that intrigue is based on the way that the spaces are designed to challenge the player—either in the form of combat or through puzzles and complex jumps. The case of *Prince of Persia* makes this clear: despite being the narrator of the game, and the visual center that we follow, the prince himself did not structure the space or create these puzzles. There are clearly two different forms of agency at work here. Seen from this point of view, we can say that the structuring that makes space meaningful and gives it a narrative impetus is the result of the work of the intrigant.

NARRATIVE GEOGRAPHIES

By this point, we are far away from what we would normally think about a theory of character. Instead, we have found ourselves positing a theory of the design of the landscape and its relationship to narration. But I would like to suggest that this is an important component of what makes an account of the compositional nature of character in digital narrative distinct. I invoked Frow's skeptical account of the relationship between characters and persons at the outset of this chapter precisely because he encourages us to think about the way that characters *do* certain things for narratives in ways that have nothing to do with our understanding of real-world persons. The fact that an attempt to understand the role of movement in digital characters has led us away from anything we would associate with print characters and into an exploration of seeing, narration, and landscape is, I think, a sign of precisely these compositional demands in the digital work.

Before I leave this topic of character movement and the digital landscape, I would like to suggest that this idea of the designed space with and within which the player must struggle has some relevance to our understanding of the spaces of non-digital texts as well. I would suggest that Said's account of the orientalist travel narrative depends on a similar tension between the observing eye and the presumed space on which it acts. In the colonialist imagination that Said analyzes, that space is structured by the culture that the European visitor strives to describe and resist. Of course, suggesting that Chateaubriand or Nerval is the intriguee when navigating the Orient in many ways simply accepts the colonial narrative in which the landscape is a hostile force to be overcome. But this association does encourage us to consider the relationship between the act of narration and the way that space exists as available to certain kinds of actions and descriptions. For all of its sophistication, postcolonial theory tends to focus on the way that discursive forces—from Anderson's "imagined communities" to Bhabha's "production of the nation as narration" (297)—bring the nation and its people into existence. As Dustin Crowley puts it in regards to Africa in particular, "Because of its history with challenging and intellectually dismantling the nation, much postcolonial criticism approaches all geographic categories and sense of place with no small amount of suspicion; even domestic and urban scales are often subject to the same erosions and transgressions as overtly contested categories like the nation" (6). In trying to describe the way that spaces might resist or deform this narrating impulse, this model has the potential to raise some interesting questions and to offer a dynamic account of space and narrative agency in other media.[11]

This dynamic interplay between narrative and landscape has attracted increasing interest at the intersection between narrative and geography. In particular, *Narrating Space/Spatializing Narrative* by Marie-Laure Ryan, Kenneth Foote, and Maoz Azaryahu, explores not just how stories construct and use spaces, but also how real-life spaces like the city and the museum are narrativized. A simple example is the way that commemorative street names can "weave history telling into the cityspace and into ordinary experiences" (141). Likewise, "point narratives" that describe historical events from a single vantage point through commemorative plaques represent an obvious way that physical locations are connected to time. And, of course, museums both construct historical narratives for visitor movement, and themselves interact with their historical locations through (at times) the repurposing of historically significant buildings and other types of sites (197).

In these cases, it is obvious that the physical landscape is both the object of narration, and a resource that shapes the kinds of stories that can be told.[12] Ryan, Foote, and Azaryahu in particular invoke Bertrand Westphal's "geocriticism" as "the investigation how fictional worlds intersect with the world

---

11. In fact, this is part of Lefebvre's critique of Foucault's *Archaeology of Knowledge:* "Foucault never explains what space it is that he is referring to, nor how it bridges the gap between the theoretical (epistemological) realm and the practical one, between mental and social, between the space of the philosophers and the space of the people who deal with material things" (4). In other words, as I take it, Lefebvre asks how these representations (imagined communities, narrated nations) are imposed on the physical space that we actually occupy.

12. Rita Raley describes some locative narratives as acknowledging "history as an active thing, a persistent framework for re-experience" (307).

of human geography in its concern for how the earth supports human cultures, how behavior is affected by the physical properties of the environment, how human activity impacts the environment, and how people experience and organize space and place" (209). One element of such a geocriticism is studying "the impact of real-world geography on the collective imagination." They cite as an example Robert T. Tally's description of Westphal's approach: "Instead of looking at the ways in which Dickens represents London in his novels, Westphal's geocritic starts with London [. . .] and then proceeds to look at various texts which attempt to represent it" (Tally 141; ellipsis in original; cited by Ryan, Foote, and Azaryahu 209). This resonates with the way that Said's travelers are responding to and seeking to reshape the Orient through their visits. Such work hopes to describe more broadly the way that organizing forces shape how individuals can occupy the landscape, and thus the kinds of stories that can be told about them.

The character/movement relationship and the way that it is implemented in digital narrative provides a framework for thinking about this dynamic between narration and the spaces that support and resist it. Further applying the language of narrator and intrigant offers a suggestive account of the tension between the constraints of space and objects, and the work of narration and description that are central to the emerging field of narrative geography.

SCALE

Movement is, then, one of the principle compositional features in the characters of digital narrative. I would like to return to Frow's book to explore a second observation that is relevant to digital characters as well: the issue of scale. Although I have largely focused on individual on-screen avatars thus far in this chapter, digital media is particularly good at representing large data sets. I noted the irony already that our focus on these individual avatars has meant that we have given this element of the presentation of persons so little attention in scholarship. Frow's book provides a framework for thinking about characters above the level of individuals. These two issues—the tool-like function of an on-screen avatar for movement, and the way that multiplicity can be represented through characters—stand out as the two most distinctive elements of characters in digital narrative, and I will argue at the end of this chapter that they are actually deeply connected.

Most of the scholarship on narrative character has focused on individuals. David Herman remarks that "narrative is a mode of representation optimally suited for person-level phenomena" (Herman et al. 127). It is for this reason that Frow's attention to the issue of scale in characterization is so refreshing. Frow begins by noting that "all theories of character are to some degree typological, invoking a limited range of kinds of person subsuming actual named characters" (107). He sees this as a fundamental dynamic in the emergence of the novel. Taking the example of Joseph Andrews, he writes:

> Yet, for all the contingency and particularity he may acquire, the lawyer remains, at the same time, a member of the class of lawyers. There is thus a continued tension between reading character as a contingent particularity and reading it as the representative of a larger class of persons. Much of the energy of the novel has gone into refusing allegorical or symbolic reference; yet to the extent that character is a structural moment of the semantic patterning of the novel, that refusal is almost impossible to achieve. (114)

Frow concludes that "novelistic character is thus a mechanism for scaling up and down between orders of generality" (114), and he evokes Lukács: the "'concrete artistic embodiment' of particularity, and the central category of realist literature, is the *type*" (115).

Frow traces the reliance on type in the novel to the broader concept of the social person drawn from Marcel Mauss. Summarizing Elizabeth Fowler, he defines the social person as a "figuration of the human that acquires a more general status of a cultural paradigm through repeated use. The concept includes such things as legal persons, civic agents, corporate entities, economic agents, kinship designations, races and ethnicities, and literary types, and it thus has close connections to the notion of social typology" (116). Such a social person embodies a certain model for social relations; it is a "personification of social bonds" (117; citing Fowler 95). Frow connects these models to a form of practical reasoning based on Bourdieu: "the formal structure of an everyday dealing with the world which operates in time, and is therefore open-ended, based on uncertainty and strategic calculation" (120). Frow offers a model, then, in which the management of scale is one of the central features of character, and a fundamental tool for practically navigating a system of social bonds.

Digital narrative is profoundly interested in the issue of scale. We might take as a simple, but very distinctly digital, example the literary uses of Twitter. Indeed, Twitter is invested in the issue of conversation at a scale far above what would normally be encountered in everyday life. Twitter itself highlights a project that shows the real-time reaction to Obama's 2014 State of the Union Address by tracking the frequency of various hashtags over the course of the speech.¹³ The result is a map of collective conversation—what, in other words, novelistic dialog would look like written not about individuals, but about a whole nation (see figure 4.2).

Although the method is very different, Twitter bots accomplish some of the same things by creating a kind of collective voice. Two included in the *Electronic Literature Collection* (volume 3) are "Two Headlines" and "The Way Bot." The former "grabs a random category and headline from Google News, then replaces the topic word with the topic from another category." The latter "scrapes Twitter for tweets that contain the phrase 'I like it when'" and then retweets the comment stripped of identifying information. In both cases, such bots capture and transform (to various degrees) the collective conversation happening on Twitter. This sense of a conversation above the scale of normal human interactions can be accomplished even when there is also some evocation of individuality. For example, the website FiveThirtyEight created the censusAmericans Twitter bot, which "tweets short biographies of Americans based on data they provided to the U. S. Census Bureau."¹⁴ An example: "I work less than 40 hrs a week. I went to college for less than a year. I'm on active duty for training in the Reserves/National Guard." While the form depends on the individual speaking *I*, the effect of the whole is to create an image of a national multitude.¹⁵

Discussion of artificial intelligence—both in video games and in current technology in general—has been dominated by individuals. This is true of the early conversation bot Eliza, but also the case with anthropomorphized digital "assistants" like Siri. What strikes me as particularly important about these uses of Twitter is that they so often create identities out of collective texts, remixing and recontextualizing snippets of online posts and news. Although it is easy to see such artificial entities as a fictional character in a relatively traditional sense—we can refer to Siri as having a certain kind of sense of humor, and joke at other times that she seems confused—the representation of collective activity and conversation is more complex. *Are* the people represented in census Americans characters? Frow sees character as always navigating a relationship between individual and type, but some of these uses of Twitter push us far to the extreme of the collective and away from the individual.

---

13. See http://twitter.github.io/interactive/sotu2014/#p1.
14. See FiveThirtyEight's explanation: https://fivethirtyeight.com/datalab/introducing-censusamericans-a-twitter-bot-for-america/.
15. See also Rita Raley's discussion of the collective quality of installations that draw on, anonymize, and publicly display text messages, "TXTual Practice."

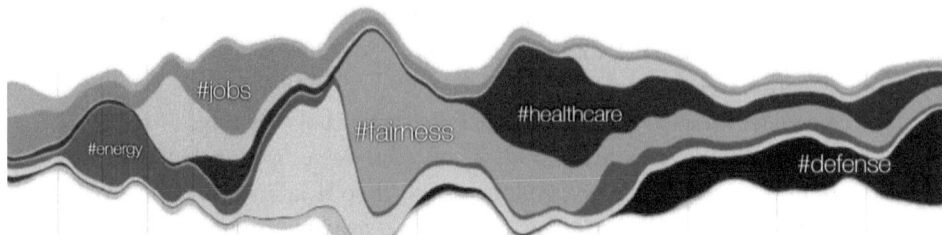

FIGURE 4.2. Hashtag use during 2014 State of the Union Address.

SCALE IN VIDEO GAMES

It is easy to see some forms of digital textuality like Twitter as shifting our sense of character far away from its traditional basis in individuality, but I would like to suggest that even in more conventional digital texts like video games, the issue of scale haunts our understanding of on-screen figures. To see why, I would like to start with a decidedly analog form of narrative. The all-but-universal model of a playable character with particular statistics that improve over time has its origin in pen-and-paper role-playing games, particularly the 1974 *Dungeons & Dragons*. This game evolved out of table-top strategy games in which players use miniature figures to represent large groups of soldiers. An illuminating example of these origins is the 1971 guidebook *Chainmail*, written by Gary Gygax (with Jeff Perren), who went on to write *Dungeons & Dragons* a few years later. This handbook is charmingly low-tech, and ultimately designed for players who want to construct their own game board and figures. These figures represent groups of units (armored foot soldiers, longbowmen, heavy horsemen, etc.), and each combat turn determines how many casualties there are in each group. In this game, the "characters" on the board obviously represent units of multiple individuals.[16]

Chainmail is particularly noteworthy because it shows an awareness of how this system would change if applied to a single combatant. Halfway through the guidebook rules for "man-to-man combat" are introduced: "Instead of using one figure to represent numerous men, a single figure represents a single man" (25). A few pages later, a "fantasy supplement" is provided giving rules for figures like elves and ogres, and we are firmly in the territory that *Dungeons & Dragons* will occupy a few years later. Reading through this combat system, we are reminded that the representation of combat in commercial

---

16. I discuss *Dungeons & Dragons*, and the mathematical basis for storytelling in the role-playing game, in *Five Strands of Fictionality*.

video games has its roots in this vision of units of multiple individuals. In the *Chainmail* rules, an attack by archers on a unit of foot soldiers may kill half of the members of that group. In *Dungeons & Dragons,* an individual character will take a certain amount of damage and lose a number of "hit points"— rather than living or dying based on a single attack. Although this approach makes sense in the case of units made up of multiple individuals—over time units will be worn down as members are killed—it does not make nearly as much sense in the case of one-on-one combat. And yet, this model of hit points is nearly universal in pen-and-paper role-playing games, as well as in commercial video games. Almost every such game frames combat as allowing the player avatar to sustain a number of injuries before dying, and thus to strategize the fight based on whether to disengage or continue.

Characters as defined by this kind of game mechanism are inherently multiple—even if the game itself denies this by representing the character as an individual—both in video and pen-and-paper games. To think about the subtle effect of character multiplicity in games, consider how the concept of character applies to a game like the *Age of Empires* Series, where the player helps to build up and defend a civilization by selecting individual characters on the landscape and assigning them tasks: gathering resources (wood, stone, food), constructing different kinds of buildings, or fighting. These characters are represented as individuals in much the same way that the *Chainmail* rules use a miniature figure to represent a whole group of soldiers of the same type. That multiplicity is implicit, and not directly represented in *Age of Empires.* It seems obvious that the on-screen characters are not just a simple representation of the whole population. Starting the game with one villager would seem to make population growth a biological impossibility, after all. Likewise, assigning workers to tasks seems incorrect in its scale; is a single peasant really going to construct an entire building? It makes more sense to assume that when we assign a worker to cut wood or construct a building, we are really directing the efforts of some portion of the society rather than controlling individuals. Read in the context of the *Chainmail* rules, it seems clear that the individual characters that we control in a game like *Age of Empires* are multiple in some way. The fact that we cannot precisely identify the correlation between the whole population and the particular characters represented on screen is itself a sign of how fundamental the issue of character scale is to these games. Indeed, both *Chainmail* and *Age of Empires* exemplify the role of scale in modeling human interactions far more directly than any of the examples that Frow discusses. The figures on screen in this game represent the relationship between different types of characters (woodcutters, archers, foot soldiers) and effective gameplay is a matter of balancing the relations between character types: players need enough general population to provide materials for their armies, but need to build up their soldiers fast enough to protect their population against other hostile civilizations. The relational nature of these groups is clearly articulated in *Understanding Video Games*, which uses the analogy of rock-paper-scissors to explain how different types of units in one of the *Age of Empires* games have the advantage over others (see figure 4.3).

This relationship between types of game units is common across a wide variety of video games, and makes clear that the primary significance is less their absolute number than their proportion. Indeed, Frow's description of character as the human-sized embodiment of more general relations is perfectly realized in games like these, since individual on-screen characters function as a kind of shorthand for more abstract conditions of the virtual population.

Although it is easy to see how scale manifests itself in civilization and battle simulations like these, I would argue that scale remains a point even when games focus on more traditional, individual figures. An interesting example of the far-reaching implications of scale as a way of embodying social relations is the popularity of squad mechanics in many games, where players assemble a group of characters that are used to complete individual missions. Most often such squads are a supplement to the player character—groups of nonplayer characters (NPCs) who are encountered over the course of the game, and who become available to accompany the player on missions. Some games keep a firm distinction between the player character and these others, giving the player only some limited ability to give directions to these helpers. In other games, though, players can take direct control of NPC companions;

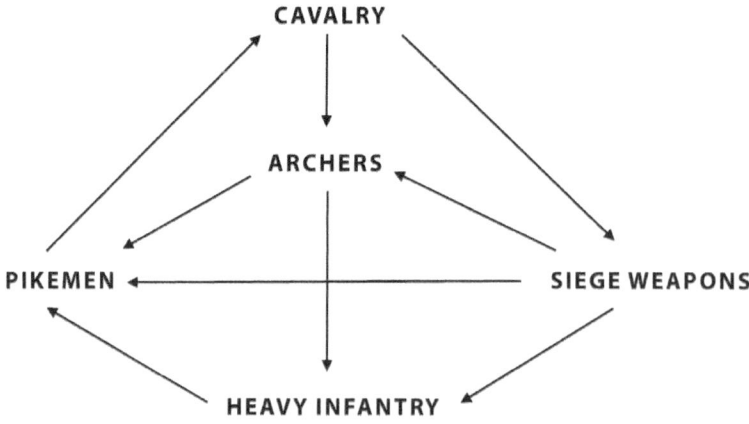

FIGURE 4.3. *Understanding Video Games*

this is the dynamic used in the influential early computer role-playing game *Baldur's Gate,* and it is carried over into subsequent games from Black Isle and Bioware. Assembling a squad of characters obeys much the same principle of population balance that we see in a game like *Age of Empires,* where we need the right mix of different kinds of capabilities. As with the ambiguously multiple nature of those characters, these squads are more a representation of a system of types than a group of individuals.

Obviously, squad games like this create fewer mimetic incoherencies than the concept of a hit-point, which seems to be the residue of an older unit model of combat applied to a single individual. But the persistence and variability of squads in games reminds us that these on-screen characters are types, whose relationship (rather than individuality) is central to effective gameplay—just as in a civilization simulation game like *Age of Empires.* This issue of character scale is also connected more subtly to the indirectness of our control of these games, which we have already observed in the previous chapter regarding event granularity. There I noted, drawing on Alexander Galloway, that many events in games are actually a combination of actions of the player and the machine. A player pushes the "reload" button on the controller, but the machine displays an elaborate series of actions as the result. Playing a game with a squad of characters most often means turning over some of your control to the computer-controlled NPCs, which is necessary precisely because the *differences* between these character types is something that must be managed within the game. Just as the player must balance farmers and soldiers in *Age of Empires,* so too must a squad of characters be balanced in other shooter and computer role-playing games. Frow helps us to see that the issue of scale emerges as a way to represent social relations; the role of those relations, in turn, means that we often have direct control over one part of the digital world at any one time.

Character scale and the issue of the indirectness of our control as a player is ironic, given that discussions of video game characters are strongly focused on individual player-controlled characters like Lara Croft. But this example reminds us that a significant portion of many games involves coordinating with multiple different agents. Indeed, we can see this particularly clearly in the *SimCity* game, which does not involve the direct control of individual characters (or groups of characters) as we have seen in *Age of Empires.* Instead, the player makes infrastructure decisions (build a road, install plumbing, designate some areas residential or commercial) and then waits for citizens to respond—moving into houses, developing property, and so on. Critics' fascination with individual, well-known video game characters and neglect for these other game elements may reflect the fact that they fit less easily into our accounts of literary character. Because Lara Croft seems like a character in a traditional novelistic sense it is easy to talk about her, and allowing her to migrate into films seems like a natural thing to do. No one ever suggests, in other words, making a movie about the woodcutters in *Age of Empires*.[17]

CONCLUSION

The two features of character that I have emphasized in this chapter—compositional function and scale—both take us far away from the way that we usually think about narrative character. It is for this reason that this chapter has ended up connecting with other elements of narrative normally seen to be outside of a theory of character: space, intrigue, and point of view. This reorientation to character is, of course, precisely why Frow's complication of the character/person relationship has provided such a valuable framework for this discussion. Digital narrative particularly helps us to see the ways that characters are less persons and more a tool to accomplish narrative and gameplay goals.

It might seem odd that this chapter has focused on two features of character when all of the others have identified a single challenge to its particular narrative concept: intrigue, the orienting space, and UI time. The two halves of this chapter are necessary and complementary, however, precisely because the *use* of character in digital narrative depends on the careful handling of scale. Digital narrative often attempts to represent enormous numbers of individuals (a national conversation on Twitter or the whole population of a civilization), while at the same time often depending on the visual point-of-view model that imitates a single human vision and is drawn from film. This is the reason *Age of Empires* depends on its ambiguously multiple figures—they are a shorthand tool for controlling the efforts of the civilization, thus showing that the issues of scale and compositional purpose are inherently linked. This ability to represent character at such a wide range of scales—sometimes as I have suggested, not quite coherently—makes digital narrative a particularly rich field for exploring the tensions in our understanding of character.

---

17. There is actually an interesting case to be made that computer-generated animation has tended to focus on individualizing mass-produced objects. Pixar's first film, *Toy Story*, focused on (normally) inanimate objects for pragmatic reasons—they are far easier to animate than objects with skin or hair. But quite a few subsequent films, from *Wall-E* to *The Lego Movie*, have focused on mass-produced objects that are nonetheless elevated to become narrative individuals. It may be that there is some residual multiplicity in such characters even when their digital production is subordinated to the filmic medium.

CHAPTER 5

Algorithm and Database in Possible Worlds Theory

MANY CRITICS have noted the relevance of possible worlds theory to digital media. As I observed in the introduction, Marie-Laure Ryan's 1991 *Possible Worlds, Artificial Intelligence, and Narrative Theory* stands out as an especially direct early exploration of the links between the computer and possible worlds theory, but a shared interest in the philosophy of language means that the fields are far more alike than it might initially seem.[1] Alice Bell's 2010 *The Possible Worlds of Hypertext Fiction* is the most extensive and direct investigation of these two fields. Bell writes,

> Possible Worlds Theory is extremely proficient at simplifying very complex ontological configurations and also has the necessary terminology for labelling the different ontological domains that are constructed by individual texts. [. . .]. While all texts construct alternatives and thereby always implic-

---

1. Amichai Kronfeld's 1990 *Reference and Computation: An Essay in Applied Philosophy of Language* explicitly articulates a concern for reference based in a speech-act model, searching for "a formal system that is rich enough to capture central concepts of communication" (156) that could be applied both to everyday speech and computer interaction. Although the modern philosophical roots of possible worlds theory can be traced back to Meinong and Russell at the beginning of the twentieth century, seminal work by Robert Howell, Hilary Putnam, Keith Donnellan, and Saul Kripke was all published in the 1970s—the same time when programming languages like Pascal, Smalltalk, and C were developed.

itly construct a modal system, hypertext fiction makes that system of reality very explicit by literalising the alternative possibilities. (25)

Hypertext is part of a broader category of what David Ciccoricco calls "network fiction." This term does not designate fiction disseminated through the internet, but rather fiction that challenges traditional ways of structuring narrative, whether in print or in digital media: "Network narratives have boundaries and limits, but they do not offer a reliable way to analyze a structural whole: in an obvious sense readers may or may not encounter all of the nodes that exist in the textual database, but less obvious is the fact that even if they do, it is unlikely that all of the possible permutations of the text will be realized" (28–9). Bell treats the challenges raised by the "database" structure of digital narrative extensively, looking at the way that we can grasp the often-inconsistent worlds projected by these narratives: "In response to the ontological shift, readers must reconsider where the characters and the worlds sit in relation to each other, causing disorientation or confusion if only temporarily. This creates a feeling of uneasiness because the reader's original relationship to the text is disturbed" (45). As Bell's and Ciccoricco's comments suggest, analysis of possible worlds in digital narrative has largely focused on how readers can make sense of stories that depend on variable events, outcomes, and reading order.

In this chapter, I will explore the database central to digital media and its relationship to possible worlds theory's account of the ontology of the fictional world. I will show that both digital media and possible worlds theory depend on a notion of the database, and that understanding the relationship between database and narrative illuminates both digital media theory and possible worlds theory.

POSSIBLE WORLDS THEORY AND THE DATABASE

To understand the role and significance of the database in possible worlds theory and digital media, I will depend on Lev Manovich's discussion of database and narrative forms, which is a central part of *The Language of New Media*. Published in 2001, Manovich's book has been the subject of extensive commentary. While many critics have challenged and corrected this opposition as simplistic, Manovich's early study set the terms for much of the subsequent work, and thus returning to this early book can help to clarify the stakes and assumptions of seeing a similarity of database in both possible worlds theory and digital media. Manovich argues that the database is an underappreciated but crucial element of contemporary structures of meaning, neglected in favor of the more traditional interest in narrative. As he writes, "database and narrative are natural enemies. Competing for the same territory of human culture, each claims an exclusive right to make meaning out of the world" (225). Narrative is embodied in the traditional media forms with which we are most familiar—such as the novel or cinema—and it is his goal to define the database and articulate what its prominence in contemporary culture means:

> Many new media objects do not tell stories; they do not have a beginning or end; in fact, they do not have any development, thematically, formally, or otherwise that would organize their elements into a sequence. Instead, they are collections of individual items, with every item possessing the same significance as any other. (218)

Writing at the end of the 1990s, it is unsurprising that Manovich's main examples of the database are the internet and CD-ROM. He sees the shift away from narrative towards the database as itself an element of the postmodern loss of narrative described by Lyotard. He says that since "the world appears to us as an endless and unstructured collection of images, texts, and other data records, it is only appropriate that we will be moved to model it as a database" and sets out to offer "a poetics, aesthetics, and ethics of this database" (219).

It is clear that Manovich is exaggerating the conflict here, in large part to keep the emerging database logic from being subordinated to more established forms. Katherine Hayles describes the narrative/database relationship as one of symbiosis,

> Rather than being natural enemies, narrative and database are more appropriately seen as *natural symbionts*. Symbionts are organisms of different species that have a mutually beneficial relation. For example, a bird picks off bugs that torment a water buffalo, making the beast's existence more comfortable; the water buffalo provides the bird with tasty meals. Because database can construct relational juxtapositions but is helpless to interpret or explain them, it needs narrative to make its results meaningful. (*How We Think* 176)

In coining the term network fiction, Ciccoricco argues that the database can essentially give rise to different kinds of narrative forms: "'narrative' and 'network' are not opposing cultural forms. Networks redistribute narrative—both in shifting the delivery model from *one-to-many* to *many-to-many* and in the sense that networks redistribute narrative elements into self-contained semantic units" (8). Manovich too recognizes that we can have a narrative experience of the database as we navigate through it. In fact, the 1990s forms that he has in mind would sometimes mimic narrative structures. He notes the case of a CD-ROM that might "simulate the traditional museum experience of moving from room to room in a continuous trajectory," but warns, of course, that "this narrative method of access does not have any special status in comparison to other access methods" (220). It is clear that Manovich sees such narrative modes of access as an artificial and even nostalgic structure being imposed on the new database form, and that his emphasis on a fundamental opposition between narrative and database is designed to help move away from these nostalgic modes.

In thinking about the database/narrative relationship, Manovich offers the concept of interface as a way to understand their fundamental similarities and differences. In new media like the CD-ROM or web pages, "the content of the work and the interface are separated" (227). We might access a particular website through one of many browsers, or even use a mobile app to pull that same data and organize it differently. In this regard, he suggests, traditional media with their narrative structure might be seen as simply one instance of what could be a more variable experience: "An interactive narrative (which can also be called a *hypernarrative* in an analogy with hypertext) can then be understood as the sum of multiple trajectories through a database. A traditional linear narrative is one among many other possible trajectories, that is, a particular choice made within a hypernarrative" (227).

This separation of interface from data source is why I feel that Manovich's theory of the database is so relevant to possible world theories as they are applied to literary texts. Possible worlds theory grows out of an interest in the problems of accounting for how references to nonexistent entities can be meaningful. Although some philosophers maintain that the best way to address the problem of such references is by appealing to a speech-act theory of language and by claiming that such references are merely pretended, possible worlds theory emerged as a more compelling explanation. Ryan's 1991 book is in many ways a magisterial synthesis that brings together the work in the field as it emerged in the 1970s and 1980s. The core of her account of fictionality is the idea of a textual universe organized by modal worlds that surround an actual world of the story. She summarizes:

> If we regard the actual world as the center of a modal system, and APWs [alternative possible worlds] as satellites revolving around it, then the global universe can be *recentered* around any of its planets. From the point of view of an APW, what we regard as the actual world becomes an alternative. We

can make conjectures about what things would be like if Hitler had won the war; conversely, the inhabitants of the world in which Hitler won the war may wonder what would have happened if the Allies had triumphed—just as they have in actuality. (18)

Once we adopt this model of possible worlds that surround the actual world, and whose perspective we can adopt as a kind of mental exercise, it is easy to account for our experience of fictionality: "For the duration of our immersion in a work of fiction, the realm of possibilities is thus recentered around the sphere which the narrator presents as the actual world" (22).

By putting the status of entities at the center of their accounts of fictionality, these philosophers and literary theorists look at texts in a way that will remind us of Manovich's database logic, which is defined by distinct objects. Ronen describes possible worlds in this way: "A world of any ontological status contains a set of entities (objects, persons) organized and interrelated in specific ways (through situations, events, and space-time). A world as a system of entities and relations, [sic] is an autonomous domain in the sense that it can be distinguished from other domains identified with other sets of entities and relations" (8). Other critics adopt the slightly broader phrasing of "state of affairs," such as Lubomír Doležel: "*Fictional worlds are ensembles of nonactualized possible states of affairs.* Fictional worlds and their constituents, fictional particulars, are granted a definite ontological status, the status of nonactualized possibles"[1] (*Heterocosmica* 16). Doležel makes clear that for him, as for Ronen, the fictional world is constituted by fictional "particulars." These particulars include objects and persons along with their states. Overall, these objects are independent of how the "interface" presents them. Thomas Pavel notes that these states of affairs are "distinct from the statements describing those states" (50). Although it might initially seem strange to refer to the written text as simply one "interface" with the fictional world, this separation of text and world is particularly important for explaining narrative worlds that encompass multiple books or even multiple media. This is especially the case in popular media franchises like *Star Wars* and *The Lord of the Rings*—in which characters, events, and settings constitute a world that reappears in multiple individual works—but it is equally the case when we speak of Sherlock Holmes and his London being represented in many different, relatively independent novels by Arthur Conan Doyle.

---

2. As with other chapters, any emphasis in quotes is from the original text, unless otherwise noted.

Fictional worlds, in this sense, are fundamentally a matter of entities. Indeed, possible worlds accounts of fictionality actually de-emphasize the narrativity to which Manovich contrasts the database. Consider how Ryan's emphasis on modality as the center of fictional worlds redefines narrativity. For Ryan, a fictional text creates a "textual actual world" which we adopt as our temporary point of view while reading. Our experience of the fictional text is a matter of exploring the possibilities that open out from this textual actual world. This can involve a variety of ways of projecting these modal worlds: "If possible worlds are constructs of the mind, we can classify them according to the mental process to which they owe their existence. [. . .] A convenient point of departure for this classification is what James McCawley calls 'world-creating predicates': verbs such as to dream, to intend, to believe, to consider, to fantasize, to hypothesize" (19). From this perspective, then, any story actually creates a "narrative universe" made up of multiple worlds with different modal relationships from what we take to be the actual world projected by the story. As Ryan writes,

> Within the semantic domain, the text may outline a system of reality: an actual world, surrounded by APWs. I regard this semantic dimension as constitutive of the narrative text. Narrativity resides in a text's ability to bring a world to life, to populate it with individuals through singular existential statements, to place this world in history through statements of events affecting its members, and to convey the feeling of its actuality, thus opposing it implicitly or explicitly to a set of merely possible worlds. (112)

When reading a fictional text, we are invited to consider the hopes and dreams of characters, what they believe to be true, what they plan for the future and imagine could have happened in the past, and so on. What strikes me as especially important in the context of Manovich's distinction between the database and narrative is that this modal theory is a way of transforming the narrative temporality that we associate with storytelling into a structure of states connected to different possible worlds. From this point of view, Ryan's theory could be seen as a way of making the objects of the text central, and treating events as largely secondary, associated with the various worlds that surround the textual actual world.

I am arguing, then, that possible worlds theory represents the application of a database logic focusing on entities to narrative texts that have traditionally been discussed in terms of plot, surprise, and resolution—of temporality, in other words. Although I am not arguing for a straightforwardly causal relationship between possible worlds theory and this database logic, it is clear that both emerge from a computational mindset that comes to prominence during the 1970s.

ALGORITHM AND POSSIBLE WORLDS

Having shown the similarities between the database and possible worlds thinking, I would like now to begin to consider how recognizing this database logic might generate insights into the dynamics of possible worlds theory as it is applied to written texts. In particular, I would like to focus on Manovich's discussion of the algorithm and its relationship to the text that is our interface with this narrative world.

I want to start with a discussion of the idea of structure in the database and possible worlds theory. Manovich notes that, in computer science, "*database* is defined as a structured collection of data" (218). Such structures can take many forms:

> Different types of databases—hierarchical, network, relational, object-oriented—use different models to organize data. For instance, the records in hierarchical databases are organized in a treelike structure. Object-oriented databases store complex data structures, called "objects," which are organized into hierarchical classes that may inherit properties from classes higher in the chain. (218)

Manovich is quick to point out that the databases of new media need not "employ these highly structured database models" (219). Websites, he notes, are usually "collections of separate elements—texts, images, links to other pages, or sites" (220). Manovich tends to treat new media database forms as largely unstructured, and to see our experience of these objects as being shaped by the way that we encounter them—such as his example of the museum CD-ROM mentioned earlier.

This issue of encounter adds complexity to the role of the database in new media. Jessica Pressman notes that "databases are not just repositories for storing data; they are structures that organize, prioritize, and shape information. Their mediation has meaningful impact on how information is processed, presented, and understood" (102). But Manovich is somewhat murky on exactly how the database is given structure. When Manovich first introduces the idea of structure in the database, he does so by treating it as a quality of the object; in an object-oriented database, for example, child objects inherit qualities from their parents. When he talks about databases in new media, however, he emphasizes the way that we can act on them: "From the point of view of the user's experience, a large proportion of them are databases in a more basic sense. They appear as collections of items on which the user can perform various operations—view, navigate, search" (219). Manovich does not pursue the potential tension between the database's structure and the operations that we can perform on it, but it is easy to see that they are related without quite being the same thing.

A crucial element of database structures in new media for Manovich is their relationship to algorithms. Manovich describes this relationship as "symbiotic" (223), but the exact way that the structure provided by the database interacts with that of the algorithm is somewhat murky. An algorithm is, of course, simply a step-by-step set of operations to be performed. Manovich introduces the concept into his discussion by using the example of the video game: "As the player proceeds through the game, she gradually discovers the rules that operate in the universe constructed by this game. She learns its hidden logic—in short, its algorithm" (222). Learning to play the game, he argues, involves "trying to build a mental model of the computer model" that will allow the player to execute the algorithm (223). Manovich argues that within contemporary computing culture the world is translated into the database and algorithm:

> The world is reduced to two kinds of software objects that are complementary to each other—data structures and algorithms. Any process or task is reduced to an algorithm, a final sequence of simple operations that a computer can execute to accomplish a given task. And any object in the world—be it the population of a city, the weather over the course of a century, or a chair, or a human brain—is modeled as a data structure, that is, data organized in a particular way for efficient search and retrieval. (223)

According to Manovich, database and algorithm work together to model the world. It seems clear, as well, that the kinds of actions that we can perform on the database are generally related to the algorithm. For example, knowing that file systems depend on nested directories of some sort means that before we can do a search we need to know that we are using the proper path. But knowing the structure of the files does not tell us everything about how to act on them, such as the availability of a wild-card operator or the degree to which the search system can use Boolean logic.

Of particular interest is Manovich's somewhat surprising turn to equate algorithm and narrative. I have already noted that many later theorists have criticized Manovich's categorical opposition between narrative and database, and this move only seems to confirm that the two are more intertwined than he will initially admit. Reading a narrative does not require us to adopt "algorithm-like behavior"—we can get to the end of a novel merely by knowing how to read and turn the pages of the book, in contrast to a video game that may require a complex understanding of movement and combat to progress. Nonetheless, he argues,

> narrative and games are similar in that the user must uncover their underlying logic while proceeding through them—their algorithm. Just like the game player, the reader of a novel gradually reconstructs the algorithm (here I am using the term metaphorically) that the writer used to create the settings, and the events. (225)

This is a provocative suggestion, even though Manovich backs off from its implications somewhat by concluding that the equation of narrative and algorithm is merely metaphorical. Although it might initially seem strange to apply the idea of an algorithm to the novel, it helps to make sense of a common phenomenon: that, when confronted with a new type of writing, readers must learn how to read these stories before they can fully enjoy them. This insight is the foundation of Peter Rabinowitz's explanation of the "rules of reading" in *Before Reading*: "These rules govern operations or activities that, from the author's perspective, it is appropriate for the reader to perform when transforming [i.e., interpreting] texts" (43).

Manovich is describing, then, a level of organization in the database that is more than just an enumeration of its objects. In possible worlds theory, Doležel describes a similarly intermediary structure when he distinguishes what he calls extensional and intentional narrative worlds. Doležel offers this contrast as a reformulation of the difference between reference and sense. He cites Kirkham: "The extension of an expression is the object or set of objects referred to, pointed to, or indicated by, the expression" (4; cited in *Heterocosmica* 136). Intension, in contrast, is defined in various ways by the philosophers and literary critics who use the term. Doležel specifically treats the texture as a quality that reveals the implied structure of values embodied in the intensional world:

> Literary texts thrive on exploiting the semantic differences of expressions with the same informational content, revealing the vacuity of the notion of intensional equivalence (synonymy). They demonstrate that intension is necessarily linked to texture, to the form (structuring) of the expression; it is constituted by those meanings, which the verbal sign acquires through and in texture. (137-8)

Doležel's example of texture is the way a narrative might refer to characters differently: by a proper name (Odysseus) or a definite description (the king of Ithaca) (139–40). From an extensional point of view the inventory of objects in the world is the same regardless of how they are referenced. However, it is easy to see how different styles of reference would subtly color the work. He gives the example of Robinson Crusoe: "Three persons of its world are given proper names—'Robinson,' 'Xury,' and 'Friday'—while all the other inhabitants are named by definite descriptions only—'my father,' 'the Portuguese captain,' 'the English captain's widow,' 'Friday's father,' and so on" (140). This textural difference reveals an intensional world that supplements its extensional one.

I find Doležel's concept of extensional and intensional narrative worlds to be powerful precisely because it gets at aesthetic patterns in the writing of the story that can sometimes be neglected in possible worlds theory's focus on entities and modalities. However, it is clear from this summary that Doležel's theory still makes entities and their states of affairs the basis of the work. He summarizes the interconnection between the intensional and extensional: "Although extensions and intentions can and must be differentiated in semantic theory, they are by definition complementary in the production of literary meaning. Extensions are available only through intensions and, conversely, intensions are fixed by extensions" (142). Indeed, Doležel suggests that "authors conceive the fictional world first as an extensional structure, inventing the story, individuating the acting persons in their properties and relationships, setting them in landscapes and cityscapes" (143). This summary nicely captures the fact that possible worlds theory imagines narrative primarily in terms of the entities that populate the world. This is clear when Doležel explains how readers reconstruct these worlds:

> The readers are presented first with the intensional structuring, since they access the fictional world through the text's texture; by information or formalized paraphrasing they translate the texture into extensional representations and thus reconstruct the extensional world structure and its parts—story, character portraits, landscapes, and cityscapes. (143)

Like Manovich, Doležel sees reading as a matter of gradually building a model of the fictional world (its database of extensional objects and the values that structure them intensionally). Precisely how the algorithm contributes to this model is somewhat vague. After all, writing a novel is hardly a step-by-step process. If we return to the example of video games, we can think of learning about its regularities, not only the mechanics that allow a player avatar to move, but also the implicit rules of enemy behavior, the types of jumps that are successful, and so on. In a novel, the equivalent of these implicit rules includes the sort of values that Doležel associates with the intensional world, but these regularities would also involve other things like patterns in character behavior, the kinds of situations in which they tend to find themselves, and so on. The metaphorical algorithm Manovich associates with fiction, then, seems to be a structure that exceeds that provided by the intensional world. In comparison, the intensional world is much closer to the way that a database might be given structure, since both concern the ordering of low-level components.

GENRE AND THE USE OF POSSIBLE WORLDS

I have focused so much on Manovich's discussion of the algorithm because it gets at something that has intuitive relevance to narrative fiction: our sense of the inherent logic of the world. The possible worlds structure of fiction obviously helps us to describe some features of their worlds: the objects and places that constitute them and the way that other possible worlds are projected by modal structures. Manovich's claim that readers (or players in a video game) intuitively grasp the logic of the narrative world strikes me as a step beyond this possible worlds description, and gets at higher-level concerns that we might describe as the "style" of the world. The concept of *style* has always been both intuitive, and yet problematic, within possible worlds theory. Doležel is quite explicit in associating literary style with the texture:

> The concept of style in general, and of literary style in particular, is hardly a rigorous concept. However, it has been useful in literary study and beyond by expressing the intuition of an organized, regulated, consistent individuality or specificity. I am tempted to define literary style in terms which, at first glance, appear almost contradictory: *Literary style is an ordered set of global regularities of texture, determining conjointly the idiosyncrasy of the literary text.* ("Literary Text" 195)

Doležel makes clear that texture helps us to recognize a characteristic ordering of the textual world. Doležel introduces this concept carefully because the idea of *style* in a fictional world might seem contradictory: worlds seem to be independent of the phrasing of the story, but we also know that we can get clues about the underlying logic of those worlds from the way that texts describe them. To take a simple example, we know that historical specificity is going to be unimportant to the fairy tale, and thus not part of the style of these worlds, in many ways: we can observe the lack of geographical names or precise dates, but we can also intuit this value from their classic opening line, "Once upon a time [. . .]."

Although Doležel's account of literary style is important, we should recognize that there are many other aspects of the style of a fictional world. I have already briefly discussed Ryan's theory of "the principle of minimal departure" in chapter 2, the rule that "we construe the alternate world of a textual universe in the same way we reconstruct the alternate possible worlds of nonfactual statements: as conforming as far as possible to our representation of" the actual world (51). In other words, when we read a novel set in modern Paris, we assume the existence of the Seine and Eiffel Tower even if they are never mentioned in the book; likewise, we do not wonder how characters get around the city because we know there are taxis and the Métro. Although the concept of minimal departure is well known, Ryan's attention to its limitations has received less attention than it deserves. She gives the example of the problematic implication that the writings of Aquinas are part of the world of "Little Red Riding Hood," and offers the observation that "the principle of minimal departure may be too powerful for most fictional genres" (53). Ryan goes on to suggest that we learn these principles through intertextuality, rejecting "the view that textual universes are created *ex nihilo,* and that textual meaning is the product of a self-enclosed system" (55). Like Rabinowitz, Ryan recognizes that stories depend on materials and forms that can be shared across different texts. Of particular importance is the way that genre influences minimal departure and guides us when we imagine fictional worlds. Genre, she argues, provides three factors: thematic focus (such as psychological, historical, or detective); stylistic filtering (which features of the worlds objects are represented, such as the idyllic); and probabilistic emphasis (the degree to which unlikely events are the focus of the story) (43–4). When we pick up a detective novel, we know that it will generally be about crime and guilt (thematic focus), that a mixture of often densely populated public and private spaces are likely to be the focus of events (stylistic filtering), and that events will be resolved logically and without appeal to extraordinary or supernatural forces (probabilistic emphasis).

Ryan's observation about the way that genres influence the nature of the fictional worlds points us to a number of textual qualities that create the impression that a particular world has a style. In *On Literary Worlds,* Eric Hayot offers a suggestive listing of the stylistic features of what he calls "worldedness." Initially Hayot's characterization of literary worlds accords with what I have been describing as a kind of database logic:

The world of a Balzac novel, for instance, is located in a time (the early nineteenth century) and a place (mostly Paris); includes certain kinds of people (the bourgeoisie; the aristocracy, their servants) and largely excludes others (the noncriminal working class); is organized around certain types of plots and social units (the family, particularly the extended family); and so on. (43)

Hayot's summary of Balzac's world could be described using a language of inventories (what spaces and characters are in the world and how are these objects organized into modalized alternative worlds) and modalities (what kinds of action are possible, required, and so on). As his discussion develops, however, Hayot becomes increasingly focused on what we might describe as matters of style. His first of six "aspects of worldedness," for example, is drawn from Auerbach's famous discussion of the stylistic difference between the *Odyssey* and the *Bible*, which of course emphasizes the degree to which each work provides detail about the world. Even more suggestive is Hayot's focus on the nature of time in Bakhtin, which he sees as describing a degree to which the world is dynamic.

Although Hayot does not emphasize the term *chronotope* specifically, it is clear that Bakhtin's concept is precisely the matter of style that seems to be a problematic part of any possible worlds theory. As we have seen in chapter 2, Bakhtin's theory describes how at different historical moments the novel imagines time and space, and how that in turn produces very different ways of representing human life. The Greek adventure novel relies on an abstract space of random events whose characters do not change or progress, for example, while the chivalric romance describes a miraculous world that puts the hero at its center and makes him "at home" and "every bit as miraculous as his world" (154). At the very beginning of this essay, Bakhtin associates the chronotope and genre:

> The chronotope in literature has an intrinsic *generic* significance. It can even be said that it is precisely the chronotope that defines genre and generic distinctions, for in literature the primary category in the chronotope is time. The chronotope as a formally constitutive category determines to a significant degree the image of man in literature as well. The image of man is always intrinsically chronotopic. (84–5)

Bakhtin's focus on genre resonates nicely with Ryan's observation about the way that genre defines the limits of minimal departure. In both of these cases, genre is a feature more general than the particular text, and helps to create in the reader a set of expectations about the way to build a world out of the particular objects and events represented explicitly. In other words, genre describes a style of our access to the represented world that cannot be equated either with the catalog of entities or the values associated with them—Doležel's extensional and intensional worlds.

Although the role of genre has gotten relatively little attention in possible worlds theory outside of Ryan's work, I think that it allows us to describe a crucial feature of the "style" of these worlds, which is related to but ultimately independent of the style of writing in the text itself. As I have already argued, the most obvious case of this is how we know to fill in gaps differently according to genre—we expect to apply the principle of minimal departure rigorously in realist fiction, and loosely in fairy tales. To appreciate the difference between the style of the text and the style of its world, we might think of postmodern reworkings of the fairy tale. In a novel like Donald Barthelme's *The Dead Father* or a story like Robert Coover's "The Magic Poker," we encounter narratives that share the fairy tale world style but whose sentence-level writing is frequently more sophisticated or whose individual scenes might be more explicitly sexual than would be conventional in such stories. We might likewise think of the way in which some genres encourage us to use them in different ways: some stories are clearly intended to develop realistic worlds (such as in science fiction), while others are designed to teach a moral lesson (such as a fable), and still others are designed to serve as thought experiments ("If one twin travels in a spaceship near the speed of light, while the other remains back on earth [. . .]"). Pavel touches on this element of the use of worlds: "Semantically, tragedy can be characterized in contrast with mythical ontologies and epic sequences of events. Myths, being narratives, are composed of chains of events; by virtue of their privileged ontology, they serve as models of intelligibility for events in the profane world" (131). In other words, the features of the fictional world lend themselves to different uses—even if the worlds themselves happen to contain the same objects and values. In this regard, Manovich's choice of the term algorithm is especially appropriate, since that term describes what is *to be done* with the objects in the database. Genre, I am arguing, helps readers to build particular types of worlds from the texture of the work, and to know to what use to put that world.

CONCLUSION

I hope to have shown that the four-part model that Manovich offers—of object, data structure, algorithm, and interface—can serve as a useful model for thinking about the structure of possible worlds in fiction. Objects and their modalities form the base of the world, and the data structure is similar to the intentional world that Doležel describes—a system by which the objects in the world are valued and given shape. The interface, obviously, is the highest level of the work, the place where we encounter the story from which we reconstruct this world. It is the equivalent of the algorithm that has largely escaped notice in possible worlds theory. I have argued that the algorithm is roughly equivalent to genre, and defines the way that a world can be imagined and used. It is the metaphorical algorithm and its relationship to genre that Manovich helps us to recognize.

In a traditional print text the interface is not as obvious as a distinct element of the work. As a result, the structure of interface/algorithm/world can remain merely implicit. In other words, by separating world and our interface with it, digital narrative encourages us to consider the relationship between a text and its world. Specifically, the emphasis on genre and the uses to which a world can be put is something that is often merely implicit in other media. My understanding of genre departs from more conventional theories that see genre simply as a form of classification—what Tzvetan Todorov describes as "discursive properties" that may appear either natural or conventional (162–3) and that may be codified historically according to the values and ideology of a particular society (164). Instead, I have followed John Frow's recent account of genre as a means "to mediate between a social situation and the text which realizes certain features of this situation, or which responds strategically to its demands. Genre shapes strategies for occasions; it gets a certain kind of work done" (*Genre* 14–15). Carolyn Miller's rhetorical account of genre particularly embodies this equation of genre and action: "Genre refers to a conventional category of discourse based in large-scale typification of rhetorical action; as action, it acquires meaning from situation and from the social context in which that situation arose" (163). I have argued that one aspect of that social context includes the actions that readers are supposed to take in building a fictional world. In this sense, genres provide guidance about what to *do* with the story, which is independent of the surface-level writing of the text itself—although one hopes as a reader that these two features of the story ultimately work together.

As in other chapters, reading narrative theory through the lens of digital media has helped us to recognize an element of that theory that has been underdeveloped. I think that recognizing how genre can perform some of the same functions as the algorithm is, somewhat surprisingly, also relevant to work on digital media itself. Throughout this book I have drawn on Jan-Noël Thon's work on transmedial narratology at some length, and I think that the role of genre would be a useful supplement to that theory. In their introduction to *Storyworlds across Media,* Thon and Ryan address transtextual media franchises as a particularly compelling instance of the independence of the world from the particular textual "interface" through which we encounter it: "Each of the sequels, prequels, adaptations, transpositions, or modifications that make up the body of these franchises spins a story that provides instant immersion, because the recipient is spared the cognitive effort of building a world and its inhabitants from a largely blank state" (1). In *Transmedial Narratology and Contemporary Media Culture,* Thon frames the issue of how we fill in the gaps as a central concern for the concept of storyworld as it moves across media. He describes the concept of the storyworld as a "transmedial concept" even though this "does not necessarily mean that storyworlds across media are all alike." In discussing storyworlds across media, he focuses on two particular qualities:

> Both narrative representations of storyworlds and these storyworlds themselves are necessarily incomplete, but recipients use their (actual as well as fictional) world knowledge to "fill in the gaps," to infer aspects of the storyworld that are only implicitly represented. This also leads us [. . .] to the observation that storyworlds—as worlds populated with characters and situated in space and time—consist not only of existents, events, and characters but also of the spatial, temporal, and causal relations between them, which are essential for understanding the various locally represented situations as part of a more global storyworld. (87–8)

Thon's discussion of storyworlds leads him to a focus on two of the qualities that I have associated with intermediary structuring concepts: the process of filling in gaps, and the style of spaces and time. My discussion of the algorithm suggests that we can add to this list the uses to which the world is put, and reframe the whole set as a matter of an intermediary structure that shapes how we imagine the world that is represented in the particular media "interface."

To Thon's account of transmedial narratives, then, I am reintroducing genre and the way that it guides our use of those worlds. Although I have emphasized the way that digital media challenged narrative theory in past chapters, this is an instance where this relationship is partially reversed. Having recognized the continuity between digital and older print media helps us to see the limitations of our theories of digital media as well. Use is also especially relevant as we think about cross-media franchises, which so often depend on varying genre in order to give readers or game players a different experience of the same narrative world. Just as different video games set in the *Star Wars* universe allow players to do different things (fly spaceships, fight with lightsabers), so too do we expect a young-adult novel and a mainstream movie set in the same world to allow the audience to do different things. No doubt different media impose different constraints and provide different affordances on narratives in these franchises, but genre also helps to guide our sense of what we can do with these different stories set within the same world. Genre and the way that it supports the imagination and use of worlds is the feature of possible worlds theory that Manovich's algorithm reveals.

This discussion has also confirmed a quality of digital media that has appeared to some degree in each chapter: a focus on the way that the particular narrative artifact allows or even demands certain kinds of actions. Sometimes the physical quality of this artifact is quite explicit—as in the case of the user interface and its participation in intrigue. In other cases, such as in this chapter, the physical design of individual digital narratives has been less important than their more abstract design. More broadly, although I have associated this issue of use with the physical (digital) device through which we encounter the text, this chapter reminds us that there are social elements like genre that shape the use of texts as well. In *How to Do Things with Videogames*, Ian Bogost argues for a wide range of possible uses of media in general, while focusing on the video game in particular. In fact, he argues that this range of uses is a partial response to the limitations of a media ecological model, since games (like all media) never simply perform one role in the ecology. Throughout this book my interpretation of use has been narrower and largely defined by the user interface. This chapter's discussion of genre makes clear, however, that Bogost is right to emphasize the way that any medium can take on a wide range of uses defined by its social context. In all of these cases, we can say that digital media extends and challenges our general narrative theories by forcing us to consider the way that these works participate in user actions and uses to which these works can be put. This chapter's analysis of the algorithm is a particularly clear and appropriate conclusion, since it shows all the ways that users must learn and apply the rules of genre.

CONCLUSION

Narrative Theory, Play, and Artifact

> People who are really serious about software
> should make their own hardware.
> —ALAN KAY[1]

THIS EPIGRAPH is a well-known remark by Alan Kay, who worked at the groundbreaking Xerox PARC laboratory, and helped to create (among many other things) object-oriented programming. Kay's observation may at first seem to have little to do with narrative theory, but he raises an important issue about the interconnectedness of the mechanical form of a device and the content that it can produce. That interconnection is especially visible and compelling in the case of digital narrative, where we are very aware of the way that changes in hardware make possible different affordances in software—from the way that the invention of the mouse made the graphical user interface practical, to the way that motion sensing in the Wii enables different forms of physical gameplay. In this conclusion, I would like to consider the relationship between theoretical play and the kind of physical artifact through which it is produced. Throughout this book I have demonstrated how programmers and designers use digital media to explore the assumptions and limits in our core narrative concepts. I want to discuss the implications of this link between play and artifactuality, the idea that varying our material interactions with a narrative medium—playing with it—is a way of exposing theoretical assumptions and their limits.

---

1. This often-quoted line is attributed to Kay's talk at the computer industry seminar Creative Think in July of 1982. See Andy Hertzfeld's account at Folklore.org, available online at http://www.folklore.org/StoryView.py?story=Creative_Think.txt.

Implicit in Kay's observation is a critique of the idea that the material conditions of a particular computing environment can disappear into a general and contentless platform for design and programming. The rise of personal computers at the end of the 1970s ushered in the assumption that most of our interactions would be with general-purpose machines that could run a variety of software that addressed widely different contexts and uses. In fact, this has never really been the case: most of the computing that we encounter on a daily basis is hardwired into specific devices, from the ATM we use to withdraw money, to the DVD player we use to watch a film, to the digital clock that wakes us up in the morning. With the rise of mobile and, most recently, wearable computing in the new millennium, we are once again more aware of the particular physical devices that we use to do our computing than we were in the age of the beige-box PC tower. Kay's observation suggests that a general-purpose computing platform depends on very special circumstances that are fragile and likely to pass quickly. When he claims that those who are "very serious" about software will want to create their own hardware, he implies that the limits of general hardware will quickly be encountered, and that it is only the least-demanding and most conventional forms of computing that can use such machines.

I think that this is relevant to narrative theory. One way to read the history of literary theory in general is as the product of just such a fragile moment of a general-purpose platform. The rise of theory as a discipline, which we can trace back to the New Critics in the 1940s for their widespread classroom practices, or to the 1970s for its broad curriculum adoption as a distinct field, constitutes a very specific moment in which a number of institutions are in place and hegemonic enough to create a sense not just of stability but even of inevitability. These include publishers, booksellers, reviewers, and universities. Like the PC of the 1990s, literature and the book form more generally felt like a stable "general platform" that is relatively neutral and unchanging. Indeed, one way to think about poststructuralism's radical critique of literary conventions—from the death of the author to Derrida's claim that there is nothing outside the text—is as a way of taking this general platform to its logical conclusion. To abstract away all of the institutional machinery of publication, audience, and composition for the sake of textuality in general is to radically undermine our understanding of that general platform from within.

In the last twenty years, we have begun to recognize the limitations of this general platform. Institutionally, the role of the university in policing the canon of literature has been problematized. Amazon and community sites like Goodreads have transformed the role of the book review. Digital publication by Amazon as well as in web-based forms of distribution has changed our sense of the book format itself, as well as raising issues of permanence, ownership, and community. In this environment, digital narrative has emerged as perhaps the emblematic media form for thinking about the nature of our roles as creator and consumer of stories. In each of the chapters of this book I have argued that the mechanics of our interaction with the story have been foregrounded and problematized. We can see that, in particular, in the splitting of narrator and intrigant in the first chapter. It is also clear in the introduction of UI time in the third chapter, and in the way that the orienting space of the computer game complements traditional settings. In each of these chapters, in other words, we find digital narrative revealing the mechanics of the narrative machines that we have been able to take for granted in the past. Digital narrative helps us to see that all delivery methods for stories are machines, and that all of those machines in turn have roles that the reader and author—as well as many others—have to occupy.

Of course, digital narrative is not the first form to draw our attention to the physical limitations of traditional print. In *Digital Modernism*, Jessica Pressman invokes I. A. Richards's observation that "a book is a machine to think with" before connecting it to McLuhan and the rise of media studies (35). It is precisely this emphasis on the physical object that has proven central to revealing the roles that readers, publishers, and authors take on in the media ecology. In fact, looking back now it is easy to see the conventional single-author codex book as the product of a relatively brief historical moment. Writing about how modern editions of eighteenth-century novels ignore their "rambunctious materiality," Janine Barchas notes, "When it comes to modern editions and reprints of the eighteenth-century novel, editorial practice has not been attentive to the genre's original appearance as a printed book, ignoring its layout, prefatory puffs, end matter, and graphic design and dismissing its punctuation and ornamentation as 'accidentals'" (6). The novel achieves its modern form during the nineteenth century, including international copyright law and a system for production and distribution of literary materials.

Already at the turn of the twentieth century this system is in flux both economically and in the erosion of the uniformity of its material embodiment. In *Institutions of Modernism*, Lawrence Rainey notes how Sylvia Beach's publication of Joyce's *Ulysses* shifted away from the common model of mass publication towards a system of elite patronage in response to concerns about the limitations of mass taste. Noting that the cheapest form of the first edition of the novel represented "almost half a month's rent for a studio in a moderately priced part of" Paris, he concludes that, as a result, "when private readers purchased copies of the first edition, they did not just buy a book, they also assumed some of the functions of patrons" (64). Rainey's focus is on the economics of Beach's publishing decisions (different editions printed on different paper at dramatically different prices), but experimentation with book design is of course a hallmark of modernism. We might think of early concrete poetry like Stéphen Mallarmé's *Un coup de dés* (1914) or Guillaume Apollinaire's *Calligrammes* (1918). Perhaps most famously, Bob Brown's 1930 manifesto "The Readies" called for a machine that would speed up reading by automatically scrolling a ribbon of print.

Viewed from this perspective, the canonical print novel—authored by a single person, printed in mass quantities, protected by copyright, and relatively independent of the particularities of the material features of its printing—is actually uncontested for a relatively brief period of time, and is perhaps best seen more as an artifact of nineteenth-century US and European culture than as a universal feature of modern life. Indeed, we might see Joyce's collaboration with Beach as another analogy to Kay's observation about controlling the machine that runs your software: Joyce is able to produce *Ulysses* only because he is able to find a new mechanism for distributing his writing, and a new economic model to support a type of work that did not have mass market appeal. As Lisa Gitelman suggests, digital media makes the negotiation of these sorts of roles both more explicit and a feature of the design of these works. In other words, digital media embodies the material decisions about the creation, distribution, and reception of narrative that, at times, appear to happen invisibly or naturally in other media.[2]

Narrative theory is particularly receptive to this kind of play. In his 1994 book, *Fictions of Discourse: Reading Narrative Theory,* Patrick O'Neill takes a step back from offering *a* narrative theory to examine narratology as itself a kind of game. He notes that narrative in general is playful and has a propensity to undermine its own story: "The central point about narrative discourse to be considered here is that, in consequence of this division [between story and discourse], discourse is always potentially subversive of its ostensibly 'natural' role as an instrument or vehicle" (4). For him, narrative theory participates in this playful, subversive logic—it is the theory to narrative's practice (31). As I noted in chapter 3, this means that "all narratives are a form of semiotic game":

---

2. For a broader critique of bibliographical models of books as self-contained, see also Johanna Drucker's discussion of books as "distributed and conditional documents": "Our conception of a book shifts from that of an autonomous object that 'contains knowledge' and to the notion it is part of a 'knowledge ecology' and exists in a co-dependent relation to the cultural systems of production/reception in which it functions" (22).

There is certainly an evident sense in which the activity of the reader of such a narrative can be seen as a form of game, a game in which, depending on various contextual constraints, certain interpretive "moves" are allowed and others are regarded as invalid. The same is even more clearly true of the author's activity as voluntary creator of the make-believe world of the narrative presented, he or she also enjoying certain freedoms and subject to certain constraints as regards particular "moves." (26–7)

And since narrative theory participates in playfulness that is at the heart of storytelling in general, it too is a game: "Within the larger game system of literary theory, that form of theory devoted specifically to narrative is itself likewise a whole system of games, played by different players in different contexts for different purposes, a system in which the rules of the individual games are similar but by no means necessarily the same" (29).

Narrative theory, perhaps more than any other area of literary studies, contains a natural orientation towards play. For all that we might want to tease the narratologist intent on adopting opaque jargon and increasingly elaborate categories for types of discourse and narration, contained in this taxonomical obsession are the raw materials for a kind of experimentation.[3] Once we have distinguished between homodiegetic and heterodiegetic narration, between the extradiegetic and intradiegetic, between simultaneous and prior narrating—just to take Genette's well-known examples from *Narrative Discourse*—we naturally are prepared to think about their possible combinations, and the way that they sort well-known narratives. This, after all, is exactly what Genette himself does in his summary chart slotting in different works into different combinations of these terms (248). Something similar happens when Mieke Bal tackles the relationship between story and discourse time—or what she calls TS for the time of the story, and TF for time of the fabula. She postulates a "norm tempo, a zero-line" where story and telling time are roughly equal, and then provides a schematic of five kinds of time ("My presupposition is that every narrative can be divided up into segments which each correspond to one of these five tempi" [102]) before going on to describe examples of each sort of time in print narrative. In each of these cases, the common inclination towards taxonomy in narrative theory lends itself to a kind of exploratory, playful thought about possible forms of narrative: what is the equivalent of slow motion in print, or summary in film?

---

3. I am defining "play" here as a meaningful and creative activity bounded by a set of rules—a definition that goes back at least to Johan Huizinga's 1950 *Homo Ludens* (11). In this case, such taxonomies are the set of rules that frame creative exploration.

Digital narrative plays with such narrative forms by adopting features of the medium that offer new combinations or forms of narrative categories. When censusAmericans tweets out the biographical information about individual census respondents (as we saw in chapter 4), it uses the medium's ability to synthesize many individual voices into a single feed that (as I argued) raises questions about scale in characterization. Likewise, when Michael Joyce creates an authorial voice that seems to know something but not everything about the digital interface with which the reader is interacting, he teases apart two sources of creative agency (the narrator and the intrigant) that are invisible in most other media. In all of these cases, digital narrative is able to take advantage of features of the artifact through which the reader encounters the story in order to raise questions about how these core ideas function.

I would like to conclude this book, however, by exploring the continuities between digital and print narrative, and to argue that we can still see in the artifactuality of the print text some opportunities for a similar playfulness. To show this, I would like to turn to two examples: the 2001 video game *Black & White,* and the frequently analyzed 1983 short story by Margaret Atwood, "Happy Endings."

BLACK & WHITE

Black & White was a much-anticipated game from developer Peter Molyneux, who had earlier achieved fame with games like *Populous* (1989) and *Dungeon Keeper* (1997). The game is best understood as a transformation of the civilization simulation genre embodied in games like *SimCity* and *Age of Empires* (discussed in chapter 4). In games like these, the player controls members of the civilization directly (*Age of Empires*) or indirectly (*SimCity*) in order to develop infrastructure, gather resources, and defend against threats. Often these threats are external—like military assaults or natural disasters—but they can also include internal problems, such as pollution or urban sprawl. Most often in games like this, the player is not represented by an in-game avatar, but instead controls resources and activities from an abstract position external to the gameworld. The remarkable anticipation about this game before its publication was the result in part of Molyneux's reputation and skill at working with the press, but also because the game clearly merged and transformed a wide variety of genres popular at the time. A contemporary review enthused, "Hugely ambitious gameplay melds realtime resource management, elements of RPG and action-adventure, beat 'em up, and Tamagotchi-style creature care in a sumptuous 3D environment" ("Black & White Review").

From my perspective, Molyneux's most interesting innovation in *Black & White* is to challenge and complicate this abstract external position for the player. Here the player interacts with the gameworld by an embodied hand, which can pick up objects and people and move them around the landscape. Doing so can be a way of reassigning these people to different tasks, but manipulating villagers requires a careful touch, since dropping them from a height will kill them. Likewise, proper manipulation of the landscape involves work to manipulate the camera and scale—players must zoom in close enough to be able to pick up an object or person accurately, but often it is easiest to move this object to its new location from a more distant perspective. In other words, the routine work of interacting with this virtual world is significantly fussier than in a traditional simulation game. It is in part for this reason that the gaming website *Gamespy* called it one of the 25 most overrated games of all time:

> The screenshots were beautiful, the giant creatures were charismatic, the premise was golden, and the technology (which allowed you to look at the whole world and then zoom ALL the way in to see a single worm wriggling in an apple) never ceased to amaze. So you can't really blame the hype for getting out of hand. The gaming world fell in love with the idea, and embraced the game with open arms when it came out.
>
> There was trouble in paradise, though. While it was a brilliant high concept, the core game was lacking. There was no way to really interact with your townspeople, short of giving them tons of resources (or hurling them about). Controls were unintuitive. ("25 Most Overrated")

This review sees these problems as design flaws, but I think that they are implicit in the premise of an embodied 3D hand as a tool to intervene in the virtual world. Just as it complicates our interface with the world, so too does it reframe our sense of how and why we *get* to control everything. *Black & White* requires the player to earn the belief and prayers of the population by behaving as a deity. The player may function benevolently and provide blessings on the world, or may inspire fear by destroying objects and killing villagers. Belief opens more of the world to control, and provides more powers for the player.

In interviews Molyneux always emphasized the moral dimension of the game, and in particular foregrounded the issue of control and consequences that so often goes unexplored in games. In a 2001 interview, he explained his thinking.

> The result is a game which says as much about the player as it does about Peter Molyneux and his team at Lionhead. "What you will realise by the time you get to the end is that there is nobody judging your actions, there is no other force, a higher god. You are completely free to do whatever you like, because you were called into the world by the prayers of the people."
>
> "Actually what is judging whether you are good or evil is the little people. And this is the philosophical point behind the game. It's sort of inspired by the saying 'if a tree falls in a forest how do you know it makes a noise.' So if you do evil things and nobody sees you do them, you don't get any more evil for it. But if you do evil things in the middle of a village and lots of people see them then you get a lot more evil. So you realise that the little people are judging you, but they've got no real power over you." (Gestalt)

Molyneux's description of this philosophical point is a bit grandiose, but it is accurate as a critique of the ideology built into many games. *Black & White* draws attention to the assumptions in traditional civilization simulation games—in particular, the idea that the player resides "nowhere" and has an unproblematic and unmediated control of this gameworld. By embodying the player as a deity who must learn the mechanics of the most basic acts in the world, Molyneux reveals how many shortcuts these games usually take. More importantly, he illuminates a certain ideological blind spot in games built around the idea of unproblematic and uninhibited control. By forcing the player behave like a deity, and by constantly judging the players' actions as good or evil, *Black & White* reveals a whole conceptual layer to these games that is usually ignored.

It should be easy to see why I find *Black & White* an appropriate digital text with which to conclude, since this work demonstrates a playful experimentation with so many narrative concepts. The game shares the challenges with some of the core narrative concerns that I have discussed in this book. In particular, the issue of scale is central, since control of the islands and its inhabitants is a central (and difficult) part of gameplay. In chapter 4 we saw that simulation games sometimes depend on an ambiguous scale where characters on-screen appear to be individuals but actually represent population groups. The same ambiguity is the case with the villagers in *Black & White*. The tension between the nominal goals of the game and the sometimes difficult mechanisms of physical operation also evokes the tension between the author and the intrigant. Indeed, one way that we can understand the somewhat problematic success of *Black & White* is as reflecting the tension between the stated goals of exploring morality embodied in the game's opening voice-over narration focused on the story content of the game and its world ("Are you a blessing, or a curse?" the narrator asks) and the difficulties introduced by the way that the player must interact with the gameworld physically. For all that those are sometimes seen merely as a failure of user interface design ("Controls were unintuitive" the retrospective noted above), in many ways it reflects the struggle to overcome the assumptions about how to design resource simulations and what it means that the player is positioning in an outside 'nowhere' space.

Black & White also effectively shows how important genre is in our understanding of these gameworlds. Indeed, one of the things that makes the game so striking is that it combines many of the expectations of the resource simulation game (gather materials, build infrastructure) with a style of interaction that evokes the one-on-one interaction between the player (or at least the disembodied hand of the player) and individual figures in the landscape. As I noted in the previous chapter, much of our focus on possible worlds has been on how they change across media. *Black & White* demonstrates yet again that an important component of world construction is our sense of what we can *do* in the world. Indeed, the game innovates precisely by combining and transforming the basic sense of agency that civilization games usually provide the player with. This game is especially noteworthy because it was developed at a time when the PC platform had emerged as the default vehicle for simulation games—as close to the neutral platform that can be taken for granted. *Black & White* transforms the rules of the civilization simulation genre by emphasizing elements of the camera and perspective that were normally seen as less relevant than they were to other genres. As a result, it provides an ideal example of the role of genre in determining the "style" of the world and the way that we can use it.

Black & White, then, takes advantage of features of its medium (the 3D landscape and camera movement) that had been largely ignored in the genre to explore how this changes the representation of agency and scale. Indeed, its publication in 2001 represented something of a peak in PC gaming, and came in the midst of the rapid improvements in 3D rendering in the late 90s and early 2000s. It is precisely the play with these technical features of the PC hardware that allowed it to adopt a different position among various genres. Molyneux's sometimes grand claims about the philosophical context of his games offer a good example of how this kind of play with the material possibilities of the form can challenge our most basic assumptions about storytelling in games. And that play is grounded in the specific, physical qualities of the artifact (PC and mouse) through which we encounter it.

"HAPPY ENDINGS"

Margaret Atwood's 1983 "Happy Endings" is a staple of the undergraduate literature classroom, and an obviously playful rethinking of the nature of plot. Atwood's story starts with the most mundane possible framework: "John and Mary meet. What happens next?" (37). Atwood goes on to generate six additional life stories for these two, from uninteresting happiness ("John and Mary fall in love and get married. They both have worthwhile and remunerative jobs which they find stimulating and challenging [. . .]" [37]), to infidelity ("Mary falls in love with John but John doesn't fall in love with Mary" [37]), illness, and natural disasters. The end of each story is the same, though, as Atwood explains: "The only authentic ending is the one provided here: *John and Mary die. John and Mary die. John and Mary die*"[4] (40).

Much more explicitly than *Black & White*, "Happy Endings" embraces its playfulness, specifically framing the story as a kind of experimentation. At several points Atwood offers the reader the chance to imagine other possibilities: "If you think this is all too bourgeois, make John a revolutionary and Mary a counterespionage agent and see how far that gets you" (40). In a stance quite similar to that of the narratologist, Atwood starts with a framework and then varies the details in order to see how this alters the narrative that results. Atwood accomplishes this by emphasizing the artifactuality of the story itself—just as we have seen *Black & White* and so many other digital texts draw attention to themselves as technical artifacts. The various possible plots are labeled by letter, and the story itself makes explicit reference to these options in a way that draws attention to them as elements of a single document that needs to be navigated: "If you want a happy ending, try A" (37), "John marries Madge and everything continues as in A" (38), "everything continues as in A, but under different names" (39). Atwood evokes the Choose-Your-Own-Adventure format and the nontraditional way you must read those narratives by turning to different sections based on reader decisions. In other words, Atwood draws attention to what we can call the navigational scheme for the text.

---

4. As with other chapters, any emphasis in quotes is from the original text, unless otherwise noted.

Obviously, Atwood's playfulness is designed to draw attention to our ideas of plot, and in particular to challenge the emphasis that we see on the story/discourse relationship in conventional narrative models. "Happy Endings" seems designed to evacuate the interest that we have in the story's causality and progression by repeating the outcomes despite changes in character and event: we see over and over again that the story events that are normally the focus of traditional storytelling do not matter to the overall arc as Atwood describes it. We can see Atwood's unconventional narrative arrangement as a way of drawing attention to what I called UI time in chapter 3—the way that we interact with the physical text to access the story and discourse time. Normally, our relationship to the forward movement of the story in the print text is unproblematic: we turn pages largely without thinking, and look forward to seeing how the events of the story will unfold. Atwood's repetition of stock plots and constant restarting of the story suspends this forward movement of time, and forces us to pay attention to our own time of navigating these multiple, overlapping stories. "Happy Endings" questions the forward movement of the text towards its resolution as the organizing principle for our experience of the story, and thus raises the possibility of other ways of interacting with these stories as a reader.

In chapter 2, I noted that one overlooked element of setting was the way in which texts can create an exterior location from which the events of the story are accessed and observed—what I called the orienting space of the story. When applied to a print text, this kind of external position can manifest itself in appeal to *use* the text in some way—from Moretti's mapping of *Our Village* to Eliot's invitation to see *Middlemarch* as a "study." Atwood clearly invokes this kind of use when she invites her readers to vary narrative details. Indeed, Atwood emphasizes the possible ways that readers might be able to use a story like this: if you want a happy ending, stay with A; if this is too bourgeois, make John a revolutionary; and so on. This way of reframing plot is relevant to the theory of character that I discussed in chapter 4 as well. Although Atwood treats her characters as traditional individuals, the repetition of these stories draws attention to how those characters function as types. Indeed, Atwood's comment that the story "continues as in A, but under different names" makes clear that the apparent individuation conferred by these names is illusory. The only genuine singularity promised in the end is provided by abandoning these kinds of plots: "That's about all that can be said for plots, which anyway are just one thing after another, a what and a what and a what and a what. Now try How and Why" (40). This emphasis on *how* and *why* promises an escape from the way that traditional narrative plots use characters as types. But, of course, this type-less storytelling is precisely what is left out of "Happy

Endings"; it seems clear that for Atwood, plots have a natural tendency to treat characters as this kind of generalized type, and that the only escape is an imagined exploration of these moments outside of plots. Truly individual characters are only possible by stepping outside of narrative, which (as we concluded in chapter 4) always implies some degree of character scale.

Atwood's "Happy Endings," then, is a good example of how traditional print texts can embrace their own artifactuality in a playful way, challenging the way that the reader is used to interacting with a story. Like the digital texts that I have analyzed in this book, this playfulness allows her to explore the tensions and assumptions in our core narrative concepts. Although digital texts generally have a wider variety of ways of drawing attention to their own artifactuality because experimentation with UI design is so much more common in digital works, that range is a matter of degree rather than kind.

This book has demonstrated that narrative theory and digital media share an embrace of play as a way to explore our assumptions about storytelling. By reminding us of the narrative artifact with which we are interacting, digital media is able to draw attention to the often much less visible work that we do when interacting with other, more familiar media forms like the book. In the process, I hope that I have offered a different way of thinking about the relationship between these two areas of scholarly and artistic practice. In the past, we have often seen narrative theory as something that can be applied effectively or unfairly to digital media, or as something that needs to be kept at arm's length to allow the digital to develop its own language and terms. Instead I hope to have shown that digital media and narrative theory are fellow travelers, exploring storytelling in their own way.

WORKS CITED

"25 Most Overrated Games of All Time." *Gamespy*. September 15–20, 2003. https://web.archive .org/web/20090415160611/http://archive.gamespy.com:80/articles/september03/25overrated/ index.shtml.

Aarseth, Espen J. *Cybertext: Perspectives on Ergodic Literature*. Baltimore: Johns Hopkins University Press, 1997.

———. "Genre Trouble: Narrativism and the Art of Simulation." *First Person: New Media as Story, Performance, and Game*. Ed. Noah Wardrip-Fruin and Pat Harrigan. Cambridge, MA: MIT Press, 2004. 45–55.

———. "A Narrative Theory of Games." *FDG '12 Proceedings of the International Conference on the Foundations of Digital Games*. New York: ACM, 2012. 129–33.

Abbott, Porter. *The Cambridge Introduction to Narrative*. 2nd ed. Cambridge: Cambridge University Press, 2008.

Aceland, Charles R. "Introduction: Residual Media." *Residual Media*. Ed. Charles R. Aceland. Minneapolis: University of Minnesota Press, 2007. xiii–xxvii.

Achituv, Romy and Camille Utterback. *Text Rain*. Installation. Smithsonian Institute, Washington, D.C., 1999.

Adams, Douglas and Steve Meretzky. *The Hitchhiker's Guide to the Galaxy*. Cambridge, MA: Infocom, 1984. Z-Code File.

Age of Empires. Redmond, WA: Microsoft Studios, 1997. CD-ROM.

Altman, Rick. *A Theory of Narrative*. New York: Columbia University Press, 2008.

Anderton, Lucy and Nicholas Robinson. *A Servant. A Hanging. A Paper House. Born Magazine*. http://www.bornmagazine.org/projects/servant/. Web.

Ankerson, Ingrid and Megan Sapnar. *Cruising*. http://collection.eliterature.org/1/works/ankerson _sapnar__cruising.html. Web.

Apple Computer, Inc. *Apple Human Interface Guidelines: The Apple Desktop Interfaces*. Reading, MA: Addison-Wesley, 1987.

Atwood, Margaret. "Happy Endings." *Murder in the Dark: Short Fictions and Prose Poems*. Toronto: Coach House Press, 1983. 37–40.

Badiou, Alain and Fabien Tarby. *Philosophy and the Event.* Trans. Louise Burchill. Cambridge: Polity, 2013.

Bakhtin, Mikhail. *The Dialogic Imagination: Four Essays.* Trans. Caryl Emerson and Michael Holquist. Austin: The University of Texas Press, 1981.

Bal, Mieke. *Narratology: Introduction to the Theory of Narrative.* 2nd ed. Toronto: University of Toronto Press, 1997.

——. "The Point of Narratology." *Poetics Today* 11.4 (1989): 727–53.

Baldur's Gate. Los Angeles: Interplay Entertainment, 1998. CD-ROM.

Barchas, Janine. *Graphic Design, Print Culture, and the Eighteenth-Century Novel.* Cambridge: Cambridge University Press, 2003.

Bardini, Thierry. *Bootstrapping: Douglas Engelbart, Coevolution, and the Origins of Personal Computing.* Stanford: Stanford University Press, 2000.

——. "Bridging the Gulfs: From Cybertext to Cyberspace." *Journal of Computer-Mediated Communication* 3.2 (1997), doi:10.111/j.1083-6101.1997.tb00069.x.

Barry, Jackson G. "Narratology's Centrifugal Force: A Literary Perspective on the Extensions of Narrative Theory." *Poetics Today* 11.2 (1990): 295–307.

Barthelme, Donald. *The Dead Father.* New York: Farrar, Straus, Giroux, 1975.

Barthes, Roland. "Introduction to the Structural Analysis of Narratives." *A Barthes Reader.* Ed. Susan Sontag. New York: Noonday, 1982. 251–95.

Bell, Alice. *The Possible Worlds of Hypertext Fiction.* Basingstoke: Palgrave, 2010.

—— and Jan Alber, "Ontological Metalepsis and Unnatural Narratology." *JNT* 42.2 (Summer 2012): 166–92.

Bhabha, Homi K. "DissemiNation: Time, Narrative, and the Margins of the Modern Nation." *Nation and Narration.* Ed. Homi K. Bhabha. New York: Routledge, 1990. 291–322.

"Black & White Review." *Edge.* March 23, 2001. https://web.archive.org/web/20120628222338/http://www.edge-online.com/reviews/black-white-review.

Bogost, Ian. *How to Do Things with Videogames.* Minneapolis: University of Minnesota Press, 2011.

Bolter, Jay David. *Writing Space: The Computer, Hypertext, and the History of Writing.* Hillsdale, NJ: Lawrence Erlbaum Associates, 1991.

—— and Richard Grusin. *Remediation: Understanding New Media.* Cambridge, MA: MIT Press, 1999.

Bordwell, David. *Narration in the Fiction Film.* Madison: University of Wisconsin Press, 1985.

Bourdieu, Pierre. *The Logic of Practice.* Trans. Richard Nice. Stanford: Stanford University Press, 1990.

——. *The Rules of Art: Genesis and Structure of the Literary Field.* Trans. Susan Emanuel. Stanford: Stanford University Press, 1996.

Brand, Stewart. "Spacewar: Fanatic Life and Symbolic Death among the Computer Bums." *Rolling Stone,* 7 Dec. 1972, pp. 50–7.

Brooke-Rose, Christine. "Whatever Happened to Narratology?" *Poetics Today* 11.2 (1990): 283–93.

Browning, Sommer and Fluorescent Hill. *Don't Be Afraid to Help Sharks.* http://www.bornmagazine.org/projects/helpsharks/. Web.

Carpenter, J. R. *In Absentia.* http://luckysoap.com/inabsentia/. June 24, 2008. Web.

Chatman, Seymour. *Story and Discourse: Narrative Structure in Fiction and Film*. Ithaca, NY: Cornell University Press, 1978.

———. *Coming to Terms: The Rhetoric of Narrative in Fiction and Film*. Ithaca, NY: Cornell University Press, 1990.

Ciccoricco, David. *Reading Network Fiction*. Tuscaloosa: The University of Alabama Press, 2007.

———. *Refiguring Minds in Narrative Media*. Lincoln: University of Nebraska, 2015.

Clark, Katerina and Michael Holquist. *Mikhail Bakhtin*. Cambridge, MA: Harvard University Press, 1984.

Coover, Robert. "The Magic Poker." *Pricksongs & Descants*. New York: Grove, 1969. 20–44.

Coover, Roderick. *Voyage into the Unknown*. http://collection.eliterature.org/2/works/coover_voyage/VoyageIntoTheUnknown/. May 25, 2008. Web.

Corneliussen, Hilde G. and Jill Walker Rettberg, eds. *Digital Culture, Play, and Identity: A World of Warcraft Reader*. Cambridge, MA: MIT Press, 2008.

Crowley, Dustin. *Africa's Narrative Geographies: Charting the Intersections of Geocriticism and Postcolonial Studies*. New York: Palgrave Macmillan, 2015.

Dannenberg, Hilary P. *Coincidence and Counterfactuality: Plotting Time and Space in Narrative Fiction*. Lincoln: University of Nebraska Press, 2008.

Darby, David. "Form and Context: An Essay in the History of Narratology." *Poetics Today* 22.4 (2001): 829–52.

Doležel, Lubomír. *Heterocosmica: Fiction and Possible Worlds*. Baltimore: Johns Hopkins University Press, 1998.

———. "Literary Text, Its World and Its Style." *Identify of the Literary Text*. Ed. Mario J. Valdés and Owen Miller. Toronto: University of Toronto Press, 1985. 189–203.

Douglas, J. Yellowlees. *The End of Books—Or Books without End? Reading Interactive Narratives*. Ann Arbor: University of Michigan Press, 2000.

Drucker, Johanna. "Distributed and Conditional Documents: Conceptualizing Bibliographical Alterities." *MATLIT* 2.1 (2014): 11–29.

Eco, Umberto. *The Role of the Reader: Explorations in the Semiotics of Texts*. Bloomington: Indiana University Press, 1979.

Emerson, Lori. *Reading Writing Interfaces: From the Digital to the Bookbound*. Minneapolis: University of Minnesota Press, 2014.

Engelfeldt-Nielsen, Simon, Jonas Heide Smith, and Susana Pajares Tosca. *Understanding Video Games: The Essential Introduction*. 3rd ed. New York: Routledge, 2016.

Ensslin, Astrid. *Literary Gaming*. Cambridge, MA: MIT Press, 2014.

Ernst, Wolfgang. "Media Archaeology: Method and Machine versus History and Narrative of Media." *Media Archaeology: Approaches, Applications, and Implications*. Ed. Erkii Huhtamo and Jussi Parikka. Berkeley: University of California Press, 2011. 239–55.

Eskelinen, Markku. "Towards Computer Game Studies." *First Person: New Media as Story, Performance, and Game*. Ed. Noah Wardrip-Fruin and Pat Harrigan. Cambridge, MA: MIT Press, 2004. 36–44.

Fasselt, Rebecca. "(Post)Colonial We-Narratives and the 'Writing Back' Paradigm: Joseph Conrad's *The Nigger of the 'Narcissus'* and Ngũgĩ wa Thiong'o's *A Grain of Wheat*." *Poetics Today* 37.1 (2016): 155–79.

Filliou, Robert. *Ample Food for Stupid Thought*. New York: Something Else Press, 1965.

Fisher, Caitlin. *These Waves of Girls*. http://www.yorku.ca/caitlin/waves/. Web.

Fizek, Sonia and Monika Wasilewska. "Embodiment and Gender Identity in Virtual Worlds: Reconfiguring Our 'Volatile Bodies.'" *Creating Second Lives: Community, Identity and Spatiality as Constructions of the Virtual*. Ed. Astrid Ensslin and Eben Muse. New York: Routledge, 2011. 75–98.

Flanagan, Mary. "Hyperbodies Hyperknowledge: Women in Games, Women in Cyberpunk, and Strategies of Resistance." *Reload: Rethinking Women + Cyberculture*. Ed. Mary Flanagan and Austin Booth. Cambridge, MA: MIT Press, 2002. 425–54.

Fletcher, Angus. *Allegory: The Theory of a Symbolic Mode*. Ithaca, NY: Cornell University Press, 1964.

Fludernik, Monika. "History of Narratology: A Rejoinder." *Poetics Today* 24.3 (2003): 405–11.

———. "Scene Shift, Metalepsis, and the Metaleptic Mode." *Style* 37.4 (Winter 2003): 382–400.

Foucault, Michel. *Discipline and Punish: The Birth of the Prison*. Trans. Alan Sheridan. New York: Vintage, 1977.

———. *Language, Counter-Memory, Practice: Selected Essays and Interviews*. Ed. Donald F. Bouchard. Trans. Donald F. Bouchard and Sherry Simon. Ithaca, NY: Cornell University Press, 1977.

Fowler, Elizabeth. *Literary Character: The Human Figure in Early English Writing*. Ithaca, NY: Cornell University Press, 2003.

Frank, Joseph. "Spatial Form in Modern Literature." *The Idea of Spatial Form*. New Brunswick, NJ: Rutgers University Press, 1991. 5–66.

Friedberg, Anne. *The Virtual Window: From Alberti to Microsoft*. Cambridge, MA: MIT Press, 2006.

Frow, John. *Character and Person*. Oxford: Oxford University Press, 2014.

———. *Genre*. 2nd edition. New York: Routledge, 2015.

Fuller, Mary and Henry Jenkins. "Nintendo and New World Travel Writing: A Dialogue." *Cybersociety: Computer-Mediated Communications and Community*. Ed. Steven G. Jones. Thousand Oaks, CA: Sage, 1995. 57–72.

Galloway, Alexander R. *Gaming: Essays on Algorithmic Culture*. Minneapolis: University of Minnesota Press, 2006.

———. *Protocol: How Control Exists After Decentralization*. Cambridge, MA: MIT Press, 2004.

Genette, Gérard. *Narrative Discourse: An Essay in Method*. Trans. Jane E. Lewin. Ithaca, NY: Cornell University Press, 1980.

Gestalt. "Peter Molyneux of LionHead Studios—Part One." *Eurogamer*. March 2, 2001. https://www.eurogamer.net/articles/i_peterm1.

Gitelman, Lisa. *Always Already New: Media, History, and the Data of Culture*. Cambridge, MA: MIT Press, 2006.

Gygax, Gary and Jeff Perren. *Chainmail: Rules for Medieval Miniatures*. 3rd ed. Lake Geneva, WI: TSR Rules, 1975.

Hanebeck, Julian. *Understanding Metalepsis: The Hermeneutics of Narrative Transgression*. Berlin: De Gruyter, 2017.

Hausken, Liv. "Coda: Textual Theory and Blind Spots in Media Studies." *Narrative across Media: The Languages of Storytelling*. Ed. Marie-Laure Ryan. Lincoln: University of Nebraska Press, 2004. 391–403.

Hayles, N. Katherine. *Electronic Literature: New Horizons for the Literary.* Notre Dame, IN: University of Notre Dame Press, 2008.

———. *My Mother Was a Computer: Digital Subjects and Literary Texts.* Chicago: University of Chicago Press, 2005.

———. *How We Think: Digital Media and Contemporary Technogenesis.* Chicago: University of Chicago Press, 2012.

——— and Jessica Pressman. "Introduction: Making, Critique: A Media Framework." *Comparative Textual Media: Transforming the Humanities in the Postprint Era.* Ed. N. Katherine Hayles and Jessica Pressman. Minneapolis: University of Minnesota Press, 2013. vii–xxxiii.

Hayot, Eric. *On Literary Worlds.* New York: Oxford University Press, 2012.

Heise, Ursula K. "Unnatural Ecologies: The Metaphor of the Environment in Media Theory." *Configurations* 10 (2002): 149–68.

Herman, David. "Introduction: Narratologies." *Narratologies: New Perspectives of Narrative Analysis.* Ed. David Herman. Columbus: Ohio State University Press, 1999. 1–30.

———. *Story Logic: Problems and Possibilities of Narrative.* Lincoln: University of Nebraska Press, 2002.

———. "Toward a Transmedial Narratology." *Narrative across Media: The Languages of Storytelling.* Ed. Marie-Laure Ryan. Lincoln: University of Nebraska Press, 2004. 47–75.

———, James Phelan, Peter J. Rabinowitz, Brian Richardson, and Robyn Warhol. *Narrative Theory: Core Concepts and Critical Debates.* Columbus: Ohio State University Press, 2012.

Higgins, Dick. *A Dialectic of Centuries: Notes towards a Theory of the New Arts.* New York: Printed Editions, 1978.

Hogan, Patrick Colm. *Narrative Discourse: Authors and Narrators in Literature, Film, and Art.* Columbus: Ohio State University Press, 2013.

Holquist, Michael. *Dialogism: Bakhtin and His World.* 2nd ed. London: Routledge, 2002.

Huhtamo, Erkki and Jussi Parikka. "Introduction: An Archaeology of Media Archaeology." *Media Archaeology: Approaches, Applications, and Implications.* Ed. Erkii Huhtamo and Jussi Parikka. Berkeley: University of California Press, 2011. 1–21.

Huizinga, Johan. *Home Ludens: A Study of the Play-Element in Culture.* Boston: Beacon, 1955.

Hutcheon, Linda. *A Poetics of Postmodernism: History, Theory, Fiction.* New York: Routledge, 1988.

Ichikawa, Scott, Thomas H. Crofts III, and James Dvorak. *Outrances. Born Magazine,* 2009. http://www.bornmagazine.org/projects/outrances/. Web.

Iser, Wolfgang. *The Act of Reading: A Theory of Aesthetic Response.* Baltimore: Johns Hopkins University Press, 1978.

Jackson, Shelley. *Patchwork Girl.* Watertown, MA: Easgate Systems, 1995. CD-ROM.

Jenkins, Henry. "Game Design as Narrative Architecture." *First Person: New Media as Story, Performance, and Game.* Ed. Noah Wardrip-Fruin and Pat Harrigan. Cambridge, MA: MIT Press, 2004. 118–30.

Johnson, John. *Information Multiplicity: American Fiction in the Age of Media Saturation.* Baltimore: Johns Hopkins University Press, 1998.

Jones, Steven E. *Roberto Busa, S. J., and the Emergence of Humanities Computing: The Priest and the Punched Cards.* New York: Routledge, 2016.

Joyce, Michael. *afternoon: a story.* Watertown, MA: Eastgate Systems, 1987. Diskette.

———. "What I Really Wanted to Do I Thought." *Of Two Minds: Hypertext Pedagogy and Poetics.* Ann Arbor: University of Michigan Press, 1995. 31–5.

Juul, Jesper. *Half-Real: Video Games between Real Rules and Fictional Worlds.* Cambridge, MA: MIT Press, 2005.

Katz, Steve. *The Exagggerations of Peter Prince.* New York: Holt, Rinehart and Winston, 1968.

Kay, Alan. "User Interface: A Personal View." *The Art of Human-Computer Interface Design.* Ed. Brenda Laurel. Reading, MA: Addison-Wesley, 1990. 191–207.

Kazemi, Darius. *Two Headlines.* http://collection.eliterature.org/3/work.html?work=two-headlines.

Kember, Sarah and Joanna Zylinska. *Life after New Media: Mediation as a Vital Process.* Cambridge, MA: MIT Press, 2012.

Kirkham, Richard L. *Theories of Truth: A Critical Introduction.* Cambridge, MA: MIT Press, 1992.

Kirschenbaum, Matthew G. *Mechanisms: New Media and the Forensic Imagination.* Cambridge, MA: MIT Press, 2008.

———. *Track Changes: A Literary History of Word Processing.* Cambridge, MA: Harvard University Press, 2016.

———. "The .txtual Condition: Digital Humanities, Born-Digital Archives, and the Future Literary." *Digital Humanities Quarterly* 7.1 (2013). http://www.digitalhumanities.org/dhq/vol/7/1/000151/000151.html.

Kittay, Jeffrey. "Descriptive Limits." *Yale French Studies* 61 (1981): 225–43.

Kittler, Friedrich A. *Gramophone, Film, Typewriter.* Trans. Geoffrey Winthrop-Young and Michael Wutz. Stanford: Stanford University Press, 1999.

Klevjer, Rune. "Enter the Avatar: The Phenomenolopgy of Prosthetic Telepresence in Computer Games." *The Philosophy of Computer Games.* Ed. John Richard Sageng, Hallvard Fossheim, and Tarjei Mandt Larsen. Dordrecht: Springer, 2012. 17–38.

Koskimaa, Raine. "Approaches to Digital Literature: Temporal Dynamics and Cyborg Authors." *Reading Moving Letters: Digital Literature in Research and Teaching.* Ed. Roberto Simanowski, Jörgen Schäfer, and Peter Gendolla. Bielefeld: Transcript, 2010. 129–43.

———. "Hypertext Fiction in the Twilight Zone." Digital Arts and Culture Conference, November 26–28, 1998, Bergen, Norway. http://cmc.uib.no/dac98/papers/koskimaa.html.

Krapp, Peter. *Noise Channels: Glitch and Error in Digital Culture.* Minneapolis: University of Minnesota Press, 2011.

Kripke, Saul A. *Naming and Necessity.* Cambridge, MA: Harvard University Press, 1980.

Kronfeld, Amichai. *Reference and Computation: An Essay in Applied Philosophy of Language.* Cambridge: Cambridge University Press, 1990.

Laclau, Ernesto. *On Populist Reason.* London: Verso, 2005.

Lang, Anouk. "Introduction: Transforming Reading." *From Codex to Hypertext: Reading at the Turn of the Twenty-First Century.* Ed. Anouk Lang. Amherst: University of Massachusetts Press, 2012. 1–24.

Laurel, Brenda. *Computers as Theatre.* Boston: Addison-Wesley, 1991.

Lefebvre, Henri. *The Production of Space.* Trans. Donald Nicholson-Smith. Oxford: Blackwell, 1991.

Lessing, Gotthold Ephraim. *Laocoön: An Essay on the Limits of Painting and Poetry.* Trans. Edward Allen McCormick. Baltimore: Johns Hopkins University Press, 1984.

Lui, Warren. "Posthuman Difference: *Traveling to Utopia* with Young-Hae Chang Heavy Industries." *Journal of Transnational American Studies* 4.1 (2012). http://escholarship.org/uc/item/7zm9r2dq.

MacCallum-Stewart, Esther and Justin Parsler. "Role-play vs. Gameplay: The Difficulties of Playing a Role in *World of Warcraft*." *Digital Culture, Play, and Identity: A World of Warcraft Reader*. Ed. Hilde G. Corneliussen and Jill Walker Rettberg. Cambridge, MA: MIT Press, 2008. 225–46.

Manovich, Lev. *The Language of New Media*. Cambridge, MA: MIT Press, 2001.

———. *Software Takes Command*. New York: Bloomsbury, 2013.

Marcus, Laura. "How Newness Enters the World: The Birth of Cinema and the Origins of Man." *Literature and Visual Technologies: Writing After Cinema*. Ed. Julian Murphet and Lydia Rainford. Basingstroke: Palgrave, 2003. 29–45.

Marino, Mark C. and Rob Wittig. "Netprov: Elements of an Emerging Form." *Dichtung Digital* 42 (2012). http://www.dichtung-digital.de/en/journal/aktuelle-nummer/?postID=577.

Mass Effect 2. Redwood City: Electronic Arts, 2010. CD-ROM.

McKeon, Michael. *The Origins of the English Novel, 1600–1740*. Baltimore: Johns Hopkins University Press, 1987.

McLuhan, Marshall. *Understanding Media: The Extensions of Man*. Cambridge, MA: MIT Press, 1994.

Miller, Carolyn R. "Genre as Social Action." *Quarterly Journal of Speech* 70 (1984): 151–67.

Miller, Rand and Robyn Miller. *Myst*. Novato, CA: Brøderbund, 1993. CD-ROM.

Montfort, Nick. *Twisty Little Passages: An Approach to Interactive Fiction*. Cambridge, MA: MIT Press, 2003.

———. "Fretting the Player Character." *Second Person: Role-Playing and Story in Games and Playable Media*. Ed. Pat Harrigan and Noah Wardrip-Fruin. Cambridge, MA: MIT Press, 2007. 139–46.

Moretti, Franco. *Distant Reading*. London: Verso, 2013.

———. *Graphs, Maps, Trees: Abstract Models for a Literary History*. London: Verso, 2005.

Morson, Gary Saul. *Narrative and Freedom: The Shadows of Time*. New Haven, CT: Yale University Press, 1994.

——— and Caryl Emerson. *Mikhail Bakhtin: Creation of a Prosaics*. Stanford: Stanford University Press, 1990.

Murray, Janet H. *Hamlet on the Holodeck: The Future of Narrative in Cyberspace*. Cambridge, MA: MIT Press, 1997.

Nelson, Jason. *i made this. you play this. we are enemies*. *Repositorium Medienkulturforschung* 4 (2013). http://www.secrettechnology.com/madethis/enemy6.html. Web.

———. *Game, Game, Game, and Again Game*. http://www.secrettechnology.com/gamegame/gamegamebegin.html. Web.

Newman, James. "The Myth of the Ergodic Video Game." *Game Studies* 2.1 (2002). http://www.gamestudies.org/0102/newman.

Nietzel, Britta. "Point of View und Point of Action—Eine Perspektive auf die Perspektive in Computerspielen." *Repositorium Medienkulturforschung* 4 (2013). https://d-nb.info/1045296538/34.

O'Neill, Patrick. *Fictions of Discourse: Reading Narrative Theory*. Toronto: University of Toronto Press, 1994.

Pac-Man. Namco. May 22, 1980. Video Game.

Parikka, Jussi. *What is Media Archaeology?* Cambridge: Polity, 2012.

Parker, Jeff. "A Poetics of the Link." *Electronic Book Review* 12 (Fall 2001). http://www.altx.com/ebr/ebr12/park/park.htm.

Pavel, Thomas G. *Fictional Worlds.* Cambridge, MA: Harvard University Press, 1986.

Pavić, Milorad. *Dictionary of the Khazars: A Lexicon Novel in 100,000 Words.* New York: Vintage, 1989.

Pearce, Celia and Artemesia. *Communities of Play: Emergent Cultures in Multiplayer Games and Virtual Worlds.* Cambridge, MA: MIT Press, 2009.

Perlin, Ken. "Can There Be a Form between a Game and a Story?" *First Person: New Media as Story, Performance, and Game.* Ed. Noah Wardrip-Fruin and Pat Harrigan. Cambridge, MA: MIT Press, 2004. 12–18.

Phelan, James. *Living to Tell about It: A Rhetoric and Ethics of Character Narration.* Ithaca, NY: Cornell University Press, 2005.

———. *Reading People, Reading Plots: Character, Progression, and the Interpretation of Narrative.* Chicago: University of Chicago Press, 1989.

———. "Rhetoric/Ethics." *The Cambridge Companion to Narrative.* Ed. David Herman. Cambridge: Cambridge University Press, 2007. 202–16.

Plants vs. Zombies. Seattle: PopCap Games, 2010. IPA file.

Pressman, Jessica. *Digital Modernism: Making It New in New Media.* Oxford: Oxford University Press, 2014.

Prince, Gerald. *A Dictionary of Narratology.* Lincoln: University of Nebraska Press, 1987.

———. "Classical and/or Postclassical Narratology." *L'Esprit Créateur* 48.2 (Summer 2008): 115–23.

Prince of Persia. Eugene, OR: Brøderbund, 1989. CD-ROM.

Propp, V. *Morphology of the Folktale.* Trans. Laurence Scott. Austin: University of Texas Press, 1968.

Punday, Daniel. *Five Strands of Fictionality: The Institutional Construction of Contemporary American Fiction.* Columbus: the Ohio State University Press, 2010.

———. *Computing as Writing.* Minneapolis: University of Minnesota Press, 2015.

Rabinowitz, Peter J. *Before Reading: Narrative Conventions and the Politics of Interpretation.* Ithaca, NY: Cornell University Press, 1987.

Rainey, Lawrence. *Institutions of Modernism: Literary Elites and Public Culture.* New Haven, CT: Yale University Press, 1998.

Raley, Rita. "TXTual Practice." *Comparative Textual Media: Transforming the Humanities in the Postprint Era.* Ed. N. Katherine Hayles and Jessica Pressman. Minneapolis: University of Minnesota Press, 2013. 5–32.

———. "Walk This Way: Mobile Narrative as Composed Experience." *Beyond the Screen: Transformations of Literary Structures, Interfaces, and Genres.* Ed. Jörgen Schäfer and Peter Gendolla. Verlang: Bielefeld: Transcript, 2010. 299–316.

Rehak, Bob. "Playing at Being: Psychoanalysis and the Avatar." *The Video Game Theory Reader.* Ed. Mark J. P. Wolf and Bernard Perron. New York: Routledge, 2003. 103–27.

Ronen, Ruth. "Space in Fiction." *Poetics Today* 7 (1986): 421–38.

———. *Possible Worlds in Literary Theory.* Cambridge: Cambridge University Press, 1994.

Ryan, Marie-Laure. *Avatars of Story*. Minneapolis: University of Minnesota Press, 2006.

———. "Introduction." *Narrative across Media: The Languages of Storytelling*. Ed. Marie-Laure Ryan. Lincoln: University of Nebraska Press, 2004. 1–40.

———. *Possible Worlds, Artificial Intelligence, and Narrative Theory*. Bloomington: Indiana University Press, 1991.

———, Kenneth Foote, and Maoz Azaryahu. *Narrativizing Space/Spatializing Narrative: Where Narrative Theory and Geography Meet*. Columbus: Ohio State University Press, 2016.

——— and Jan-Noël Thon. "Storyworlds across Media: Introduction." *Storyworlds across Media: Toward a Media-Conscious Narratology*. Ed. Marie-Laure Ryan and Jan-Noël Thon. Lincoln: University of Nebraska Press, 2014. 1–21.

Saba, Kfar. *The Way Bot*. http://collection.eliterature.org/3/work.html?work=the-way-bot.

Said, Edward. *Orientalism*. New York: Vintage, 1979.

Scholes, Robert and Robert Kellogg. *The Nature of Narrative*. London: Oxford, 1966.

Scholz, Bernhard F. "Bakhtin's Concept of the 'Chronotope': The Kantian Connection." *The Contexts of Bakhtin: Philosophy, Authorship, Aesthetics*. Ed. David Shepherd. Amsterdam: Overseas Publishers Association, 1998. 141–72.

Seay, Allison and Felipe Hefler. *House Fire*. Born Magazine, 2009. http://www.bornmagazine.org/projects/house_fire/. Web.

Shaw, Adrienne. *Gaming at the Edge: Sexuality and Gender at the Margins of Gamer Culture*. Minneapolis: University of Minnesota Press, 2014.

Short, Emily and Liz Daly. *First Draft of the Revolution*. http://collection.eliterature.org/3/work.html?work=first-draft-of-the-revolution. Web.

Simanowksi, Roberto. "Reading Digital Literature: A Subject between Media and Methods." *Reading Moving Letters; Digital Literature in Research and Teaching. A Handbook*. Ed. Roberto Simanowski, Jörgen Schäfter, and Peter Gendolla. Bielefeld: Transcript, 2010. 15–28.

Slusser, George and Tom Shippey, eds. *Fiction 2000: Cyberpunk and the Future of Narrative*. Athens: University of Georgia Press, 1992.

Sommer, Roy. "The Merger of Classical and Postclassical Narratologies and the Consolidated Future of Narrative Theory." *Diegesis* 1 (2012). https://www.diegesis.uni-wuppertal.de/index.php/diegesis/article/view/96/93.

Stanzel, F. K. *A Theory of Narrative*. Trans. Charlotte Goedsche. Cambridge: Cambridge University Press, 1984.

Stone, Jon. *The Monster at the End of This Book*. Ill. Michael Smollin. New York: Golden Book, 1971.

Tally, Robert T., Jr. *Spatiality: The New Critical Idiom*. New York: Routledge, 2013.

Tetris. Alameda: Spectrum HoloByte, 1987. Diskette.

Thon, Jan-Noël. *Transmedial Narratology and Contemporary Media Culture*. Lincoln: University of Nebraska Press, 2016.

Todorov, Tzvetan. "The Origin of Genres." *New Literary History* 8 (1976): 159–70.

Tronstad, Ragnhild, "Character Identification in World of Warcraft: The Relationship between Capacity and Appearance." *Digital Culture, Play, and Identity: A World of Warcraft Reader*. Ed. Hilde G. Corneliussen and Jill Walker Rettberg. Cambridge, MA: MIT Press, 2008. 250 63.

Turkle, Sherry. *Life on the Screen: Identity in the Age of the Internet.* New York: Simon and Schuster, 1995.

Uncharted: Drake's Fortune. San Mateo, CA: Sony, 2007. DVD-ROM.

Wake, Paul. "Life and Death in the Second Person: Identification, Empathy, and Antipathy in the Adventure Gamebook." *Narrative,* 24.2 (May 2016): 190–210.

Walsh, Richard. "Who is the Narrator?" *Poetics Today* 18.4 (1997): 495–513.

Ware, Chris. *Building Stories.* New York: Pantheon, 2012.

Wasser, Audrey. *The Work of Difference: Modernism, Romanticism, and Production of Literary Form.* New York: Fordham University Press, 2016.

Watt, Ian. *The Rise of the Novel: Studies in Defoe, Richardson and Fielding.* Berkeley: University of California Press, 1957.

Weizenbaum, Joseph. *Computer Power and Human Reason: From Judgment to Calculation.* San Francisco: W. H. Freeman, 1976.

White, Hayden. "The Problem of Change in Literary History." *New Literary History* 7 (1975): 97–111.

Wittig, Rob and Mark C. Marino. "Occupy the Emotional Stock Exchange, Resisting the Quantifying of Affection in Social Media." *Humanities* 6.33 (2017). www.mdpi.com/2076-0787/6/2/33/pdf.

Woloch, Alex. *The One vs. the Many: Minor Characters and the Space of the Protagonist in the Novel.* Princeton: Princeton University Press, 2003.

Zen Bound. Secret Exit. February 24, 2009. IPA file.

Zoran, Gabriel. "Towards a Theory of Space in Narrative." *Poetics Today* 5 (1984): 309–35.

Zuern, John David. "Temporality of Digital Works." *The Johns Hopkins Guide to Digital Media.* Ed. Marie-Laure Ryan, Lori Emerson, and Benjamin J. Robertson. 482–6.

INDEX

Aarseth, Espen, 1, 2, 10–12, 26, 35–37, 78–79, 90, 101

Abbott, Porter, 26–27, 76

Absalom, Absalom! (Faulkner), 39

action in digital media, 15–16, 19–20, 31, 36, 83–84, 94, 147; compared to other media, 31, 71–73, 139, 150; player vs. machine actions, 46–47. *See also* point of action, space: movement in games

Adventure, 7, 8

afternoon (Joyce), 10–11, 34–37, 41–42, 48, 82–83, 86, fig. 1

Age of Empires, 117–19, 144

Alber, Jan, 5, 6

algorithm, 127–31

allegory, 102–3

Altman, Rick, 105–10

Amazon.com, 140–41

Ample Food for Stupid Thought (Filliou), 91

Anderson, Benedict, 112

Arteroids (Andrews), 18–19

Assassin's Creed Syndicate, 107

audience: authorial vs. narrative, 27–28, 32–35, 48; characterized, 39–40; homodiegetic vs. heterodiegetic, 28

Auerbach, Erich, 133

avatar, 80–81, 90, 94–97

Azaryahu, Maoz, 112–13

Badiou, Alain, 76n2

Bakhtin, Mikhail, 53, 64–67, 71, 73, 76n2, 133–34

Bal, Mieke, 3, 4, 76, 77, 143

Baldur's Gate, 54, fig. 2.1

Balzac, Honoré de, 132–33

Barchas, Janine, 141

Bardini, Thierry, 10n9, 94

Barry, Jackson, 3

Barthes, Roland, 2, 6, 7

Beach, Sylvia, 141–42

Bell, Alice, 41, 79, 121–22

Bhabha, Homi K., 112

Black & White, 144–48

Blombren, Lance, 69

Bogost, Ian, 137

Bolter, Jay David, 14–15, 54

Bordwell, David, 3

Bourdieu, Pierre, 23, 114

Brand, Stewart, 9

Building Stories (Ware), 72

Calligrammes (Apollinaire), 142

Canty, Daniel, 69

CD-ROM, 12, 123–24, 127

censusAmericans, 115

Chainmail, 116–17

Chambers, Ross, 25

character, 93–120; compositional role, 98, 101, 105; as multiple in games, 116–19; "playing" a character in games, 40; as puppet, 101–5; scale in, 113–20, 146; and social bonds, 114; structuralist vs. humanist, 98; as type, 114. *See also* space: movement in games

Chatman, Seymour, 2–4 8–9, 25–27, 29, 38 106n9

Choose Your Own Adventure novels, 30, 78–79

chronotope, 53, 60–61, 65–67, 71, 133–34

Ciccoricco, David, 37–38, 94, 122, 123–24

Clark, Katerina, 65, 66

cognitive mapping, 53

computing: hard drive, 11; history of, 7–8; object-oriented programming, 139; personal computers, 140, 147–48; programming languages, 84–86; 121n1

Un coup de dés (Mallarmé), 142

Croft, Lara, 96, 119

Crowley, Dustin, 112

Cruising (Ankerson and Sapnar), 84–85, 86, fig. 3.2

"Daisy Miller" (James), 72

Dannenberg, Hilary, 77n3

database, 122–30

Dawson, Paul, 28–29

The Dead Father (Barthelme), 134

Deadline (Blank), 101

deconstruction, 140

description, 106

Dickens, Charles, 99

Dictionary of the Khazars (Pavić), 50

digital media: definition, 2n2; in the history of narrative theory, 6; as metamedium, 12. *See also* media, idleness

distant reading, 71–72

Divine Comedy (Dante), 102–3

Doležel, Lubomír, 125, 129–32

Donnellan, Keith, 121n1

Don't Be Afraid to Help Sharks, 57

Douglas, J. Yellowlees, 34–35, 42

Drucker, Johanna, 142n2

Dungeon Keeper, 144

Dungeons & Dragons, 116–17

electronic literature, 18–19

Eliza, 10, 115

Emerson, Caryl, 65

Emerson, Lori, 16, 20, 80–81

Engelbart, Douglas, 10

Ensslin, Astrid, 81n4

event, 75–92; in computer programming, 84–86; defined in narrative, 76; granularity, 89–91, 119

The Exagggerations of Peter Prince (Katz), 91

film: accessed as DVD, 92; implied author in, 29, 38; narrator in, 3–4, 29; and point of view, 99–100, 106n9

First Draft of the Revolution (Short), 87–88

Fizek, Sonia, 95n2

Flanagan, Mary, 96

Fletcher, Angus, 102–3

Fludernik, Monika, 5, 6

following, 105–10

Foote, Kenneth, 112–13

Foucault, Michel, 33, 112n11

Fowler, Elizabeth, 114

Frank, Joseph, 53

The French Lieutenant's Woman (Fowles), 32

Friedberg, Anne, 54n1

Frow, John, 93–94, 97–99, 114, 135

Galloway, Alexander, 46–47, 91, 119

Game, Game, Game, and Again Game (Nelson), 80–82, fig. 3.1

game rules, 31

Game Studies, 1n1

Genette, Gérard, 28, 77, 82, 94, 143

genre, 38, 131–35

geocriticism, 112–13. *See also* space: narrative geographies

Gitelman, Lisa, 17, 19–20

glitch, 86

Goodreads, 140–41

Google Glass, 20
Google Maps, 68–70, 110
Graetz, Martin, 7
Grusin, Richard, 14–15

habitus, 23
Hammurabi, 101
"Happy Endings" (Atwood), 148–50
Hausken, Liv, 5n6
Hayles, N. Katherine, 17–18, 19n16, 42–43, 123
Heise, Ursula, 15
Herman, David, 4, 5, 53, 64–65, 89–90, 113–14
Hertzfeld, Andy, 139m1
Heyot, Eric, 132–33
Higgins, Dick, 14
Hitchhiker's Guide to the Galaxy, 10, 40–41, 51
Hogan, Patrick Colm, 28–29
Holquist, Michael, 65, 66
Hopscotch (Cortázar), 50
House Fire, 83, 86
House of Leaves (Danielewski), 33, 50
Howell, Robert, 121n1
Huhtamo, Erkii, 17n15
Huizinga, Johan, 143n3
Human Interface Guidelines, 8
hyperlink, 30–31, 78

i made this. you play this. we are enemies (Nelson), 57, fig. 2.6
IBM MT/ST, 7
idleness in computing, 87–89
If on a Winter's Night a Traveler (Calvino), 39–40
implied author/reader, 25–51
In Absentia (Carpenter), 68–71, 110n10, fig. 2.8
In Dubious Battle (Steinbeck), 33
interactivity, 78. *See also* action in digital media
interface, 19–20, 77–81; human interface guidelines, 8; vs. narrative and database, 124, 134–35
intermedia, 14

intrigue, 26, 35–51; and gameplay space, 110–12; in print texts, 49–51; and narration, 44; unreliability, 48–49
iPad, 20

Java, 85–86
Johnson, John, 13
Jones, Steven, 7n8
Joyce, Michael, 11. *See also afternoon*

Kant, Immanuel, 65–66
Kay, Alan, 8, 139–40, 142
Kellogg, Robert, 99
Kembler, Sarah, 16
Kirkham, Richard L., 129
Kirschenbaum, Matthew, 7, 11, 12n13
Kittay, Jeffrey, 106
Kittler, Friedrich, 12, 17
Klevjer, Rune, 7n7, 94–95
Koskimaa, Raine, 81–82
Krapp, Peter, 86n5
Kripke, Saul, 93n1, 121n1
Kronfeld, Amichai, 121n1

Laurel, Brenda, 7–8, 15
Lefebvre, Henri, 112n11
The Lego Movie, 120n17
Lessing, Gotthold, 14n14
Licklider, J. C. R., 10n9
Lord of the Rings, 67, 69n3, 125
Lord of the Rings Online, 104–5, 109–10
ludology, 1n1, 11, 12n11
Luesebrink, Marjorie, 81

"The Magic Poker" (Coover), 134
Manovich, Lev, 1, 12, 99, 100, 122–31
Marino, Mark, 88–89
Mass Effect 2, 55, fig. 2.2
Mauss, Marcel, 114
McKeon, Michael, 22–23
McLuhan, Marshall, 13–14, 141
Media: archaeology, 16, 72–73; multimedia, 12–13; residual, 16; theory, 13–18. *See also* digital media

metalepsis, 79
Middlemarch (Eliot), 72, 149
Miller, Carolyn, 135
Mitford, Mary, 71
Molyneux, Peter, 144–46
The Monster at the End of This Book, 49–51
Montfort, Nick, 7, 40
Moretti, Franco, 71–72, 149
Morrowind, 46–48, figs. 1.4, 1.5
Morson, Gary Saul, 65, 76n2
Murray, Janet, 1
My Documents, 11
"My Last Duchess" (Browning), 27
Myst, 88

narration, 25–51: cybernetic, 37–38; filmic, 3–4; omniscient, 28; in painting, 29; in video games, 45–46. *See also* intrigue
Narrative: affordances, 5–6; and algorithm, 128–29; and database, 122–24; framed, 108–11; point narratives, 112; "some" vs. "a" narrative, 108–9; transmedial, 6, 79–80, 97, 135–36
narrative theory: history, 2–6; post-classical, 4–5
Neitzel, Britta, 59, 94–95
Nelson, Theodor, 10n9
netprov, 88–89
network narrative, 122–24
Newman, James, 96n4
newness, 20–24
novel: history of, 22–23

Obama, Barak, 114–15
O'Neill, Patrick, 76–77, 142–43
The Oregon Trail, 101
Outrances (Ichikawa, Crofts, and Dvorak), 43–44, 83, figs. 1.2, 1.3

Pac-Man, 54
Pale Fire (Nabokov), 50
Parikka, Jussi, 16–17
Parker, Jeff, 30

Patchwork Girl (Jackson), 10, 42–43, 48, 56
Pavel, Thomas, 93n1, 98n6, 125, 134
Perlin, Ken, 95–96
Phelan, James, 25, 27, 32–34, 39–40, 98n6
Plants vs. Zombies, 48–49, 51
play, 129–50
point of action, 59, 94–95, 97. *See also* action in digital media
point of view, 94, 99–101, 105–6, 120
Populous, 144
possible world theory, 121–37; style in, 131–34
post-colonial theory, 111–12
Pressman, Jessica, 19n16, 141
Prince, Gerald, 5n5
Prince of Persia: The Sands of Time, 101–2, 107–8
principle of minimal departure, 62–63, 132–34
publication: digital, 140–41; in modernism, 141–42; serial, 92n8
Punday, Daniel, 11n10, 12n12, 116n16
Putnam, Hilary, 121n1

Rabinowitz, Peter, 27, 32–34, 129
Rainey, Lawrence, 141–42
Raley, Rita, 89n7, 112n12, 115n15
Rehak, Bob, 99n7
remediation, 14–15, 17
Richard, I. A., 141
Ronen, Ruth, 60, 70
Russell, Steve, 7, 9
Ryan, Marie Laure: 5–6, 9–10, 30, 42, 62–63, 76, 112–13, 121, 124–26, 132, 133–34. *See also* principle of minimal depature

Said, Edward, 103–4, 111–12
Scholes, Robert, 99–100
Scholz, Bernhard, 65–67
script (in narrative theory), 89–90
SCUMM utility, 38
A servant. A Hanging. A Paper House (Anderton and Robinson), 57, fig. 2.7
setting, 60. *See also* space
Shaw, Adrienne, 96n3

Sherlock Holmes, 125
SHRDLU, 7
Simanowski, Roberto, 19n16
SimCity, 119–20, 144
Sloane, Mary Jane, 101
Sommer, Roy, 4–5
Space: cognitive approaches, 64–65; in computer interfaces, 54, 59; constructedness of, 63–64; movement in games, 101–5, 109–11; in narrative, 53–73; narrative geographies, 111–13; primary vs. orienting, 54–59; in theater, 63
Spacewar, 7–9
Stanzel, F. K., 8–9, 25, 99
Star Wars, 67, 125
Stephenson, Neal, 19
Storyspace: 10–11, 42
Super Mario Bros., 46–47

Tally, Robert T., 113
Tetris, 57, 86, fig. 2.4
Text Rain (Achituv and Utterback), 89
Thackeray, William Makepeace, 99
These Waves of Girls (Fisher), 30
Thon, Jan-Noël, 6, 45–46, 79–81, 94, 107–8, 135–37
time in narrative: compared to database, 126–27; interactive, 82; order, duration, and frequency, 77, 143; story vs. discourse time, 75–77, 142–43; user interface time, 81–84. *See also* event
Todorov, Tzvetan, 135
Toy Story, 120n17
travelogue, 103–4, 111–12
Tristram Shandy (Sterne), 39
Tronstad, Ragnhild, 96n3
Turkle, Sherry, 95
Twine, 38
twitter, 115–18
"Two Headlines" (Kazemi), 115

Ulysses (Joyce), 141–42
Uncharted: Drake's Fortune, 102, fig. 4.1
Unity game engine, 38
user interface, 35, 46, 54, 75, 85, 91–92; and embodied interaction, 89; in print, 31, 91–21; 49–50; problems in *Black & White*, 145–48. *See also* time: user interface time

VAS (Tomasula), 33
Victory Garden (Moulthrop), 10
Voyage Into the Unknown (Coover), 56, 59, fig. 2.5

Wake, Paul, 90
Wall-E, 120n17
Walsh, Richard, 28
Wasilewska, Monika, 95n2
Wasser, Audrey, 21n17
Watt, Ian, 22
"The Way Bot" (Brody), 115
webyarns.com, 32
Weizenbaum, Joseph, 10
Westphal, Bertrand, 112–13
White, Hayden, 20–21
Whorf, Benjamin Lee, 10n9
Wiener, Norbert, 10n9
Wiitanen, Wayne, 7
Wittig, Rob, 88–89
Woloch, Alex, 98n6

Xerox PARC, 139
Xerox Star, 11

Young-Hae Heavy Industries, 83, 88

Zen Bound, 55, fig. 2.3
Zoran, Gabriel, 60–64, 70
Zork, 8, 9, 40
Zuern, John David, 81–82
Zylinska, Joanna, 16

THEORY AND INTERPRETATION OF NARRATIVE
JAMES PHELAN, PETER J. RABINOWITZ, AND KATRA BYRAM, SERIES EDITORS

Because the series editors believe that the most significant work in narrative studies today contributes both to our knowledge of specific narratives and to our understanding of narrative in general, studies in the series typically offer interpretations of individual narratives and address significant theoretical issues underlying those interpretations. The series does not privilege one critical perspective but is open to work from any strong theoretical position.

Playing at Narratology: Digital Media as Narrative Theory by Daniel Punday

Making Conversation in Modernist Fiction by Elizabeth Alsop

Narratology and Ideology: Negotiating Context, Form, and Theory in Postcolonial Narratives edited by Divya Dwivedi, Henrik Skov Nielsen, and Richard Walsh

Novelization: From Film to Novel by Jan Baetens

Reading Conrad by J. Hillis Miller, edited by John G. Peters and Jakob Lothe

Narrative, Race, and Ethnicity in the United States edited by James J. Donahue, Jennifer Ann Ho, and Shaun Morgan

Somebody Telling Somebody Else: A Rhetorical Poetics of Narrative by James Phelan

Media of Serial Narrative edited by Frank Kelleter

Suture and Narrative: Deep Intersubjectivity in Fiction and Film by George Butte

The Writer in the Well: On Misreading and Rewriting Literature by Gary Weissman

Narrating Space / Spatializing Narrative: Where Narrative Theory and Geography Meet by Marie-Laure Ryan, Kenneth Foote, and Maoz Azaryahu

Narrative Sequence in Contemporary Narratology edited by Raphaël Baroni and Françoise Revaz

The Submerged Plot and the Mother's Pleasure from Jane Austen to Arundhati Roy by Kelly A. Marsh

Narrative Theory Unbound: Queer and Feminist Interventions edited by Robyn Warhol and Susan S. Lanser

Unnatural Narrative: Theory, History, and Practice by Brian Richardson

Ethics and the Dynamic Observer Narrator: Reckoning with Past and Present in German Literature by Katra A. Byram

Narrative Paths: African Travel in Modern Fiction and Nonfiction by Kai Mikkonen

The Reader as Peeping Tom: Nonreciprocal Gazing in Narrative Fiction and Film by Jeremy Hawthorn

Thomas Hardy's Brains: Psychology, Neurology, and Hardy's Imagination by Suzanne Keen

The Return of the Omniscient Narrator: Authorship and Authority in Twenty-First Century Fiction by Paul Dawson

Feminist Narrative Ethics: Tacit Persuasion in Modernist Form by Katherine Saunders Nash

Real Mysteries: Narrative and the Unknowable by H. Porter Abbott

A Poetics of Unnatural Narrative edited by Jan Alber, Henrik Skov Nielsen, and Brian Richardson

Narrative Discourse: Authors and Narrators in Literature, Film, and Art by Patrick Colm Hogan

An Aesthetics of Narrative Performance: Transnational Theater, Literature, and Film in Contemporary Germany by Claudia Breger

Literary Identification from Charlotte Brontë to Tsitsi Dangarembga by Laura Green

Narrative Theory: Core Concepts and Critical Debates by David Herman, James Phelan and Peter J. Rabinowitz, Brian Richardson, and Robyn Warhol

After Testimony: The Ethics and Aesthetics of Holocaust Narrative for the Future edited by Jakob Lothe, Susan Rubin Suleiman, and James Phelan

The Vitality of Allegory: Figural Narrative in Modern and Contemporary Fiction by Gary Johnson

Narrative Middles: Navigating the Nineteenth-Century British Novel edited by Caroline Levine and Mario Ortiz-Robles

Fact, Fiction, and Form: Selected Essays by Ralph W. Rader, edited by James Phelan and David H. Richter.

The Real, the True, and the Told: Postmodern Historical Narrative and the Ethics of Representation by Eric L. Berlatsky

Franz Kafka: Narration, Rhetoric, and Reading edited by Jakob Lothe, Beatrice Sandberg, and Ronald Speirs

Social Minds in the Novel by Alan Palmer

Narrative Structures and the Language of the Self by Matthew Clark

Imagining Minds: The Neuro-Aesthetics of Austen, Eliot, and Hardy by Kay Young

Postclassical Narratology: Approaches and Analyses edited by Jan Alber and Monika Fludernik

Techniques for Living: Fiction and Theory in the Work of Christine Brooke-Rose by Karen R. Lawrence

Towards the Ethics of Form in Fiction: Narratives of Cultural Remission by Leona Toker

Tabloid, Inc.: Crimes, Newspapers, Narratives by V. Penelope Pelizzon and Nancy M. West

Narrative Means, Lyric Ends: Temporality in the Nineteenth-Century British Long Poem by Monique R. Morgan

Understanding Nationalism: On Narrative, Cognitive Science, and Identity by Patrick Colm Hogan

Joseph Conrad: Voice, Sequence, History, Genre edited by Jakob Lothe, Jeremy Hawthorn, James Phelan

The Rhetoric of Fictionality: Narrative Theory and the Idea of Fiction by Richard Walsh

Experiencing Fiction: Judgments, Progressions, and the Rhetorical Theory of Narrative by James Phelan

Unnatural Voices: Extreme Narration in Modern and Contemporary Fiction by Brian Richardson

Narrative Causalities by Emma Kafalenos

Why We Read Fiction: Theory of Mind and the Novel by Lisa Zunshine

I Know That You Know That I Know: Narrating Subjects from Moll Flanders *to* Marnie by George Butte

Bloodscripts: Writing the Violent Subject by Elana Gomel

Surprised by Shame: Dostoevsky's Liars and Narrative Exposure by Deborah A. Martinsen

Having a Good Cry: Effeminate Feelings and Pop-Culture Forms by Robyn R. Warhol

Politics, Persuasion, and Pragmatism: A Rhetoric of Feminist Utopian Fiction by Ellen Peel

Telling Tales: Gender and Narrative Form in Victorian Literature and Culture by Elizabeth Langland

Narrative Dynamics: Essays on Time, Plot, Closure, and Frames edited by Brian Richardson

Breaking the Frame: Metalepsis and the Construction of the Subject by Debra Malina

Invisible Author: Last Essays by Christine Brooke-Rose

Ordinary Pleasures: Couples, Conversation, and Comedy by Kay Young

Narratologies: New Perspectives on Narrative Analysis edited by David Herman

Before Reading: Narrative Conventions and the Politics of Interpretation by Peter J. Rabinowitz

Matters of Fact: Reading Nonfiction over the Edge by Daniel W. Lehman

The Progress of Romance: Literary Historiography and the Gothic Novel by David H. Richter

A Glance Beyond Doubt: Narration, Representation, Subjectivity by Shlomith Rimmon-Kenan

Narrative as Rhetoric: Technique, Audiences, Ethics, Ideology by James Phelan

Misreading Jane Eyre: *A Postformalist Paradigm* by Jerome Beaty

Psychological Politics of the American Dream: The Commodification of Subjectivity in Twentieth-Century American Literature by Lois Tyson

Understanding Narrative edited by James Phelan and Peter J. Rabinowitz

Framing Anna Karenina: Tolstoy, the Woman Question, and the Victorian Novel by Amy Mandelker

Gendered Interventions: Narrative Discourse in the Victorian Novel by Robyn R. Warhol

Reading People, Reading Plots: Character, Progression, and the Interpretation of Narrative by James Phelan

www.ingramcontent.com/pod-product-compliance
Lightning Source LLC
Chambersburg PA
CBHW020739230426
43665CB00009B/497